BORDERLINE

BORDERLINE
DEFENDING THE HOME FRONT

VINCENT VARGAS

ST. MARTIN'S PRESS
NEW YORK

Certain names have been changed.

First published in the United States by St. Martin's Press, an imprint of St. Martin's Publishing Group

BORDERLINE. Copyright © 2023 by Vincent Vargas Inc. All rights reserved. Printed in the United States of America. For information, address St. Martin's Publishing Group, 120 Broadway, New York, NY 10271.

www.stmartins.com

Designed by Omar Chapa

Library of Congress Cataloging-in-Publication Data is available upon request.

ISBN 978-1-250-28557-7 (hardcover)
ISBN 978-1-250-28558-4 (ebook)

Our books may be purchased in bulk for promotional, educational, or business use. Please contact your local bookseller or the Macmillan Corporate and Premium Sales Department at 1-800-221-7945, extension 5442, or by email at MacmillanSpecialMarkets@macmillan.com.

First Edition: 2023

10 9 8 7 6 5 4 3 2 1

To my parents: You are the reason I have the foundation that I stand on today, and your wisdom continues to guide me. I am forever in your debt for your dedication to us. I hope to prove that to you through my growth as a man, father, and husband.

The byproduct of loving my kids has always been success. They are the reason and the motivation for all I do. In that effort, I have learned that my love for them is better expressed when I am engaged in their lives and not just a source of monetary support.

I would not have accomplished all that I have in my life without the unwavering support from my best friend, my loving wife. Thank you, I love you all.

CONTENTS

FOREWORD BY JOCKO WILLINK

The Border. This is the line that defines our nation. It is the boundary within which our rights and freedoms are protected as United States citizens. Within this boundary, we trust that we have freedom, safety, and security to the greatest extent possible. But that freedom, safety, and security exists only because of the service and sacrifice our military, law enforcement officials, fire departments, and first responders make every day. However, out of all those men and women in uniform, there is only one group whose sole function is to protect our borders: the Border Patrol.

When I moved to San Diego in 1991 in my journey to become a Navy SEAL, I discovered the critical and complicated role Border Patrol played in defending our nation's security. I saw with my own two eyes the complexity of the border. It is a place of international bonding, a place where people come to seek the American dream, and a place where commerce and culture combine. But it is also a vulnerable place of exploitation, illegal drugs, human trafficking, extreme violence, and illegal immigration. Like the millions of Americans living in border cities, I understood that our populace relies upon the Border Patrol agents to negotiate this delicate environment, not only protecting us from the evils of the world, but also protecting our reputation as a beacon of freedom and justice.

The September 11 attacks changed everything for all of us. As the entire military began what would become two decades of constant war, the Border Patrol was also ramping up homeland security and counterterrorism efforts on the home front. While the long-term mission of the Border Patrol has always been to detect and prevent, new terrorist threats required the Border Patrol to adapt and answer the call of a nation in harm's way.

But the story of the Border Patrol and its agents has received little fanfare. Not many Americans truly understand the depth and breadth of their mission, the continuous struggles they face, or the day-to-day sacrifices these brave men and women make.

Borderline gives us a look into border security and the Border Patrol through the eyes of a dedicated professional. Vince Vargas takes us through the steps he took to become a Border Patrol agent, from the intense training to the special operations missions. He not only explains daily Border Patrol life and culture but also shares his approach and attitude while on duty. Similar to specialized military schools, the Border Patrol has a dynamic, challenging training curriculum that teaches agents to survey the border lands and then track, apprehend, and process migrants who have crossed illegally. This requires that agents learn how to both care for scared children traveling alone and—in the same night, perhaps even at the same time—contend with dangerous criminals looking to smuggle, steal, exploit, and kill. This dichotomy—of being combative while remaining empathetic—often puts agents' lives at risk. The harsh environment of the arid desert, the desperation of people seeking a new life, and the cruelty of smugglers and criminals make for a grim and bleak environment, one with many moral dilemmas. Vince has seen all aspects of this convoluted chaos; the perspective he gives in this book is insightful and informative, and it should be mandatory reading for anyone that wants to understand the border challenge we confront as a country. In the face of this wretchedness, Vince volunteered for BORSTAR, Border Patrol's Search, Trauma, and Rescue team, out of his desire to save lives.

Borderline is also a book about leadership. Every operation—tracking smugglers, halting illegal immigration, and rescuing people in danger—poses its own unique risk. Decisions must be made. Action must be taken. That is what we see from Vince and his fellow agents. They aggressively execute mission after mission. They stay in control of their emotions. They detach in high-pressure situations.

For leaders, balancing these dichotomies is challenging—to be decisive yet forgiving, to execute the mission while prioritizing people, to care but never be overwhelmed by emotion. Knowing when and where to hold the line is a struggle. When I directed advanced training for the SEAL teams, I purposefully created stressful situations to train SEAL leaders in taking a step back, detaching from the chaos in dynamic situations, and controlling their emotions. Border Patrol must also do this. At a moment's notice, they might switch from confronting violent lawbreakers to patiently helping innocent children with life-threatening medical issues. To do this they balance their emotions and their logic, their aggression and their empathy, their instinct for survival and self-preservation and their deepest humanity. This is a challenge for anyone in any profession. But that is what Border Patrol agents do, every day.

Vince's perspective is unique not only because of his experience as a Border Patrol agent but also because he is an Army Ranger, a family man and father, and a Mexican American. As the grandson of a Mexican immigrant, he understands how the enticement of opportunity compels immigrants to illegally enter America. But as a Ranger, he has seen the patriotic sacrifices our men and women have made for this country and recognizes the need to protect them. But most of all, he knows the distinct depth of affection in parenthood and understands the sacrifices a parent would make for the future of their children. These four vantage points often contradict each other. But these contradictions are what makes Vince an honorable soldier, agent, leader, and human being.

While *Borderline* allows us to see the job of a Border Patrol agent from Vince's point of view, it also expands our understanding of the complexities of border security and immigration policy. Vince's explanations demand that we reassess everything we've been told about the border. Through the lens of his experiences, we can see the problems and solutions more clearly. He presents analogies that force us to reevaluate, like equating the security of our house to our homeland. These analogies allow us to detach from the political debate and see the issues from another viewpoint. He also combats the misinformed media portrayals of the Border Patrol by offering a more nuanced perspective of the job. The media sometimes vilifies these men and women on our front lines. But Vince challenges this misinformation about the Border Patrol. He tells the parts of the story that are often left untold: how agents routinely rescue stranded and threatened migrants; how agents put the duties of the job above their personal lives; how the Border Patrol is a critical part of Homeland Security's counterterrorism tactics and strategy, just like the FBI, the CIA, and the military. The existence of the Border Patrol isn't a political sentiment—it is an absolute necessity.

I served overseas in combat missions, and I have written books to share my experiences and lessons learned. But there are many incidents that have occurred on our border that need to be shared as well. Vince Vargas has stepped up to do just that. This book passes on an insider's viewpoint, his perspective, and his knowledge. It allows us to better understand the border and its challenges and garner a deeper respect for the men and women who protect it. Finally, this book offers us the opportunity to take these lessons of leadership and life and apply them to make us better leaders and people.

Thanks for writing this, Vince.
Jocko

BORDERLINE

INTRODUCTION

I was a Border Patrol agent, and I am proud to have been one. While I took off my uniform in 2015, I still self-identify as a member of the U.S. Customs and Border Protection Agency (the organization containing the U.S. Border Patrol) and watch with great pride at how the men and women I helped train and mentor perform the organization's vital and dangerous mission today.

However, while my heart swells with pride as I watch these professionals carry out their often-hazardous duties, it also hurts because some Americans have latched onto ill-informed media reports that take a disrespectful view of this career field and these hardworking agents. That is one reason why I wrote this book: to provide readers with an insider's account of America's Border Patrol.

As a former U.S. Army Ranger who saw combat in Iraq and Afghanistan and one who has since retired from military service, I have a loyalty to the U.S. military and I keep a close eye on military matters. That is why I find it astonishing that most Americans have a basic understanding of what the U.S. military does, even if that understanding is based solely on what they see on their network or cable broadcasts or what they read in print or on the internet. I don't know why my fellow citizens follow our "away game" U.S. military matters so closely to try to understand how we deal with our adversaries yet have virtually no knowledge of what goes on in the "home game" of protecting our borders. Today's Border Patrol agents act as a last line of defense to keep weapons, drugs, and other contraband, as well as undocumented people, from crossing into the United States.

This would be less puzzling if the Border Patrol were a new agency, but it is one that has been around for almost a century. My purpose in writing this book is not to provide you with a full history of the Border Patrol—others have already done that—but rather to share with you my personal experiences as a Border Patrol agent to help you understand what we do to protect Americans.

Growing up in California's San Fernando Valley only a few hours' drive from the Mexican border, I had a general knowledge that there were people charged with guarding our borders, and I often saw the mint-colored Border Patrol vehicles in and around San Diego during family trips between Southern California and Northern Mexico. But back then I never fully understood what they actually did. I suspect that those of you reading this are in the same boat as I was as a kid.

What we know today as the U.S. Border Patrol has a proud history of service to our nation dating back to 1924. Although changes like the immigration policies and the implementation of tech that has impacted nearly every aspect of its operations, the basic values that helped shape the Border Patrol in the early years—professionalism, honor, integrity, respect for human life, and a shared responsibility—have remained strong. These values are what make me proud to have been a Border Patrol agent.

Even as a child, I was acutely aware of the tremendous increase of illegal migration to America in the 1990s. The Border Patrol responded to this surge by increasing manpower as well as implementing modern technology, including some of the most advanced military-grade devices, such as infrared night-vision scopes, seismic sensors, and a modern computer processing system that help the Border Patrol locate, apprehend, and process those crossing into the United States illegally.

In an effort to bring a level of control to the border, the U.S. government established Operation Hold the Line, which proved to be an immediate success. Border Patrol agents concentrated in specific areas and armed with the best technology available provided a show of force to potential illegal border crossers.

Operation Gatekeeper was implemented in an effort to reduce illegal entries into San Diego, California. A national strategic plan was introduced alongside Operation Gatekeeper, setting a course for future Border Patrol action. With illegal entries at a more manageable level, the Border Patrol was able to concentrate on other areas, such as establishing anti-smuggling units and search-and-rescue teams such as BORSTAR (Border Patrol Search, Trauma, and Rescue). You'll hear more about BORSTAR later in this book.

Homeland security became a primary concern of the nation after the terrorist attacks of September 11, 2001. Border security became a topic of increased interest in Washington, DC, resulting in a doubling of the Border Patrol workforce and an equal increase in resources. Lawmakers reconsidered funding requests and enforcement proposals as they began to reassess how to monitor our nation's borders. In March 2003, the Department of Homeland Security (DHS) was established, and the U.S. Border Patrol became part of the U.S. Customs and Border Protection Agency, a component of the DHS.

Today, the U.S. Border Patrol continues its efforts to control our nation's borders with the prioritized mission of preventing terrorists and terrorist weapons—including weapons of mass destruction—from entering the United States. While the Border Patrol has changed dramatically since its inception in 1924, its primary mission remains the same: to detect people trying to illegally cross our borders and apprehend them. Border Patrol agents put their lives on the line in defense of their fellow Americans, and a number of them have paid the ultimate price in the line of duty.

Few Americans understand the full scope of this mission and what Border Patrol agents—approximately twenty thousand in active service—must accomplish around the clock. The Border Patrol is specifically responsible for patrolling nearly six thousand miles of Mexican and Canadian land borders as well as the coastline surrounding the Florida peninsula and the island of Puerto Rico.

Often, the border is a barely discernible line in uninhabited deserts, canyons, or mountains. Today, the Border Patrol utilizes a variety of equipment and methods to accomplish its mission in such diverse terrain. Electronic sensors are placed at strategic locations along the border to detect people or vehicles entering the country illegally. Video monitors and night-vision scopes are also used to detect illegal entries. Agents patrol the border in vehicles, aboard boats, and on foot. In some areas, the Border Patrol even employs horses, all-terrain motorcycles, and bicycles.

During my time as a Border Patrol agent, I always tried to integrate new technology into my daily activities in order to stay one step ahead of those who would do the nation harm. The Border Patrol continues its technological upgrade today as new generations of agents develop innovative ways to integrate contemporary innovations into field operations. Divisions within the Border Patrol are creating new and specialized technology that holds increasing potential to assist agents in fulfilling their mission.

This new technology is needed to aid Border Patrol agents holding the line to keep the nation secure. As I said at the outset, these few pages are not intended to provide you with a comprehensive history of the Border Patrol or to tell you everything the agency is doing today.

My primary goal in writing this book is to help you understand what the Border Patrol does to protect America today. For those of you wanting more on the Border Patrol's current operations and future focus, I highly recommend reading the "2022–2026 U.S. Border Patrol Strategy," which you can find at this link: https://www.cbp.gov/border-security/along-us-borders/strategy.

When I decided I wanted to write this book, it was solely based on the fact that I felt the role of the Border Patrol was not understood by the vast majority of the American public. The media has focused on the Border Patrol's role in immigration enforcement as a tool to sway votes left or right. But the fact that the Border Patrol exists isn't a political decision. It is a necessity in order to protect and guard our borders against illegal entry.

The majority of people don't even have a basic understanding of what the Border Patrol does. Some only know of the images of a Border Patrol agent on a horse, allegedly whipping illegal Haitians crossing the border of Del Rio, my old sector. One example of what people should know about the Border Patrol, in one of the most horrifying active shooter events in our history, is when a tactical BORTAC unit was the one finally able to gain entry to Robb Elementary School in Uvalde, Texas, and take down the shooter. I am enormously proud of the fact that my former BORSTAR team provided the first medical care on the scene, providing lifesaving interventions for many of the children that had been wounded.

These are the two dramatically different perspectives of the Border Patrol held by the American public, highlighting that there is vastly more heat than light on what the Border Patrol does for America, as well as for the desperate people who seek a better life here. I hope that once you finish reading this book you will have a more nuanced understanding of your Border Patrol.

I hope that the nuanced understanding that comes from

the perspective of being a Hispanic Border Patrol agent deepens your understanding of this organization. Indeed, people often ask me: "How can you be Hispanic and also want to be a Border Patrol agent?" I want to answer this honestly without some editor changing my words or trying to make me sound greater than I am.

I believe 100 percent in what America stands for. It truly is the land of opportunity. Just because a bad actor from a certain demographic makes a wrong choice does not mean that the choice should reflect poorly on the founding ideologies of America. Additionally, there seems to be a large number of people in America who are naïve as to what the immigration law is and why it needs to be enforced.

I want to remind everyone reading this book that one reason we must protect our borders is that people want to gain access to the opportunities and privileges that most Americans take completely for granted. Millions of people want to enter our country. Our current laws state that they must follow the specified immigration process to arrive here legally.

Are you ready for more? Join me for an insider's account of my time with the Border Patrol. Hold on—this will be a hell of a ride, and one that starts with one of the most notorious prison breaks and manhunts in American history.

PROLOGUE

There is an old saying that I remember from my childhood days: "You make plans, and God laughs." I got up on a hot June morning in 2015 with big plans for the day. I was organizing a birthday party for my daughter, Star, and was on the phone ordering everything I would need. I had missed so many of her birthdays during my years serving as an Army Ranger in the 75th Ranger Regiment, as a prison guard, and as a Border Patrol agent. Now she was turning ten, and I wanted to go big and make up for years of missed parties.

It was going to be the biggest party I had ever thrown for her—our neighbors in El Paso, Texas, were all invited to our home for the celebration. The theme was Hawaiian luau, and I planned on getting some coconut-shell bras and grass skirts for the girls and myself as well as a bounce house. However, in the time before the party, news stories began appearing about two convicts—both jailed for murder—who had escaped from the Clinton Correctional Facility in Dannemora, New York.

I remember thinking: *Whoever is chasing those dudes had better be ready for a fight; they won't surrender meekly.* But I also figured that because they had been on the run for about five days and the trail had likely gone completely cold, our Border Patrol unit wouldn't be called up for support. In the back of my mind, I knew that President Barack Obama was a huge supporter of law enforcement agencies and that, in addition to the FBI, he would likely bring a host of federal agencies to track down these men—but not us.

Then God started laughing. My cell phone chirped—it was my team leader, Chris Voss. He said in a cool, calm voice: "Hey brotha, we got the call. We're being activated to track down two escapees from the Clinton Correctional Facility. Grab your gear and get to the office within the hour."

A thousand thoughts immediately coursed through my brain, especially whether I would be able to succeed in this mission. But these lingered only a few seconds—I was ready. I'm not fatalistic, but I always know that any mission could be my last. The fear that I would never see my kids again was always present, but this was the lifestyle I had lived for so long, and I somehow always just managed to rip the Band-Aid off and focus on the mission—because if I did my job well, I was coming home. This is what I signed up for.

I had two priorities: get my kit packed up and get out the door on time, and attend to my kids. I told my oldest daughter, who was twelve at the time, to hold down the fort while I was gone. Arrangements had already been made, as I knew I would be gone for a while. Our team had been activated before, but somehow this felt different. It felt imminent. I kissed my kids and told them I was going to work, but I didn't make a big deal about it. Above all else, I didn't want them to worry. Keep things normal. All that said, if you ask me today to describe the toughest part of being a Border Patrol agent, this was it: knowing that you may not see your kids again.

We trained rigorously for this kind of scramble, so "packing my kit" was actually a methodical process that I had prepared for. I had a government vehicle—a Chevy Tahoe—that was assigned to me. It was outfitted with lockboxes and tough boxes for guns and other items I needed for both the tactical and medical aspects of my job. In many ways, that Tahoe was my office.

As I watched my home disappear in my truck's rearview mirror, I began to compartmentalize. I had done the best I could to help my kids not worry about me. Now I needed to ensure that I was mentally, physically, and emotionally ready for this mission so that I wouldn't let my teammates down. I replayed my brief conversation with Chris in my mind. My overriding thought was this: *If Chris was leading our team, we were in good hands.* Like me, he was a former Army Ranger, and he was universally admired throughout the Department of Homeland Security as a leader who got the job done and also took care of his people.

I took an assessment of what I had in my "office." I had two rifles and two pistols, plenty of ammo, flashlights, and tactical equipment, all standard issue for Special Operations Border Patrol agents. We all knew that we might wind up in a gunfight, and we were confident we had the right gear. But more importantly, since I was BORSTAR (Border Patrol Search, Trauma, and Rescue). I was the designated team medic with all the medical gear needed for an extended mission. I was trained to ensure that whomever I needed to treat—friend or foe—got the lifesaving care they needed.

As I raced toward the Border Patrol SOG (Special Operations Group) office on Fort Bliss Army base, I mentally inventoried my medical gear. I had come up with a plan a few years earlier to divide my gear into three levels: a fanny pack with just enough equipment for urgent needs, such as treating a gunshot wound (stopping the bleeding, fixing the breathing); a three-day pack-out carried in a backpack with more gear and a lightweight hasty stretcher for emergency transport; and a larger bag with major gear like oxygen and neck collars. I prayed that I wouldn't have to use any of this on my teammates.

I arrived at our facility and found what I expected: no chaos, no flailing, just Chris and the rest of the team coolly reading the OPORD (Operations Order, an official document detailing our orders) for the mission. Though no one said it, we were all thinking the same thing: *If the convicts escaped days ago and we were being called in to use our special tracking skills and hunt these murderers down, then local, state, and national law enforcement agencies were getting desperate.*

The OPORD had all the usual blocking and tackling that most law enforcement agencies use. That was good as far as it went. But we needed to hear from our Border Patrol leader—Chris's boss, before we headed out the door. He didn't disappoint us. His charge to us was pretty straightforward, and he cleared up the information that news reports had either left out or gotten wrong: Two prisoners at the maximum-security Clinton Correctional Facility, Richard Matt and David Sweat, were discovered missing during an early morning bed check. Matt was serving twenty-five years to life, and Sweat was serving life without parole, both for murder. The two prisoners had dug a tunnel out of the prison with tools obtained from an employee at Clinton. As a former prison guard, hearing that last bit of information made my stomach churn.

We grabbed our gear and headed out the door, jumped into a waiting truck, and drove toward an airfield a short distance away. We clambered onto a private jet and settled in for the long flight to the airport in Plattsburgh, New York, not far from the Clinton Correctional Facility. Some people think that on a flight like this we would be pumping each other up, just like an athletic team would do. It is just the opposite. Whether it's a military mission, like the ones I was on during my years as an Army Ranger, or a Border Patrol SOG mission, we are mostly quiet. If we do talk, we make off-topic jokes to ease our minds and put a damper on any nervousness we might be feeling. It is the calm before the storm.

On this flight I just wanted to sleep, because I knew that once we arrived in New York we would be busy. But before I drifted off, I compartmentalized two equally important thoughts: my love for my kids and what a blessing it would be if I survived this mission and was reunited with them, and my love for my teammates and my resolve not to let any of them down. I knew that before we landed I would need to park these thoughts of my family deep in the recesses of my brain and focus only on my teammates.

We landed, and things went into overdrive. We jumped into

waiting vehicles and headed for the command center that had been created to deal with the crisis. On the way there, we drove by the Clinton Correctional Facility. It was like something from an old movie: The prison dominated the entire city, just like a medieval castle dominated a small town. *Creepy* was the first thought I had as I looked at the prison's massive walls.

The command center was about what we all thought it would be. It was in a local high school gymnasium, and when I entered, I saw exactly what I expected: a boatload of FBI agents and officers from every state and local law enforcement agency you could name. I remember thinking: *I hope to hell someone is in charge of this group.*

To be fair, all of these law enforcement officials were working resolutely with a common purpose: to track down Richard Matt and David Sweat before they murdered someone as they fled to freedom. I remember thinking that most of these professionals did basically the same thing but that our Border Patrol team was there because we were unique: We brought a level of tracking skills no one else possessed. Looking at how long these convicts had been on the run, I knew that we were needed—and badly.

1

MAKING THE JOURNEY TO THE BORDER PATROL

My father, Carlos Vargas, was a former Marine. He came from nothing, living in the Bronx, and then moved to Echo Park in Los Angeles when he was fourteen. My father made some of what he would call "knucklehead choices" that ultimately resulted in him joining the military. He turned his life around, from a street kid to a Jarhead, eventually translating what he learned in the service into a career in the Los Angeles Fire Department. His work ethic and fierce love for his family intimidated me but also inspired me. I had much to live up to, and failure was never an option.

I was raised playing sports in an effort to keep me off the streets and from potentially falling into gangs. I had fallen in love with baseball and had hopes to someday become a professional baseball player. I graduated high school and had played on a few junior college teams, and eventually transferred to a university. At this point in my life, I had to make a choice to put baseball behind me. I made some decisions that, in hindsight, weren't really conducive to my goal of becoming a professional baseball player. I lost a full-ride athletic scholarship to Brescia University by becoming academically ineligible, and in addition, around that time I found out I was expecting a little girl. It was time to hang up my spikes and find a way to support my daughter Isabella. Her future was my new mission.

My brother JR was the one who really planted the seed to join the military. He told me: "Your life is all over the place; maybe joining the military is a good option for you. It worked for Dad." At first, his words offended me. I had plans and dreams, and I didn't feel like I was all over the place; I was just finding my path. But I soon realized the wisdom in his words, that the service really was the best option. I had to provide for Belle's needs and make sure she had benefits like insurance.

If I was going to join the Army, I knew I wanted to be in Special Operations based on what the recruiters told me, but also because I had seen *Black Hawk Down*. Watching that movie was the first time in my young adult life that I considered joining the military. I wondered if I had the courage to take the fight to the enemy like the brave soldiers in the film.

I have always been an athlete. I never had any trouble doing anything physically demanding. I was confident—I felt like there was nothing that could be too difficult for me or that I could not accomplish. I have always challenged myself in every aspect of life: to be a good man, to be a great dad, and to excel in sports. Now I was going to be transitioning into a career field that was my only option and I had to find a way to make it work. For myself, for my daughter, and for my future.

I finally decided that I wanted to be an Army Ranger. I studied the reputation of the Rangers throughout history—which went back as far as the history of this country. I wanted to be part of that lineage. People told me that Ranger training was one of the hardest things the Army had to offer. I signed up at the MEPS (Military Entrance Processing Station) in Louisville, Kentucky, in April 2003. My date to ship out was October 16, 2003. I was classified RGR 11X (Ranger Contract with Infantry Identifier). This is the job designated by the alphanumeric system. An infantryman was an 11 series. The X was an open contract depending on the outcome of the soldier's path. The RGR referred to Ranger Regiment. This means Airborne School would be attached as long as I continued along the pipeline after basic training. If at any point someone would have failed any part of the training, the alphanumeric code would change to identify what their job would eventually become.

Basic training was an interesting journey that was just a look under the hood of what the military had to offer me. Next was Airborne School, a three-week course that teaches soldiers the techniques involved in parachuting from airplanes and landing safely for combat operations.

After graduating from Airborne School, I was "politely" introduced to what was to come during the RIP (Ranger Indoctrination Program) on a one-mile march carrying most of my gear and being bludgeoned by verbal uppercuts that made me question my choice to even join the Ranger Battalion. If this was just a taste of what's to come, I was becoming increasingly nervous.

Once I graduated from RIP and headed to the Ranger Battalion, I was ready to hop onto my first deployment.

Once arriving to my unit, I had learned so much about myself already. I was a twenty-three-year-old Private First Class and I was becoming a well-rounded professional soldier—more than just a baseball player. Within forty-five days of joining Ranger Battalion, I was preparing to deploy to Afghanistan. While in Afghanistan, if I wasn't on a mission, eating chow, or in the gym, I had nothing to do but think. I knew going in that being an Army Ranger wasn't my lifelong career choice, and I was already thinking about what I would be doing once I mustered out of the Army. I had started taking EMT classes before joining the military, so following my father's footsteps into the fire department was a constant thought as far as a career choice.

One day, while sitting in a squad room in Afghanistan, a few of us started talking about what we wanted to do after we got out of the Army. I mentioned the fire department. Everyone had their normal cop or firefighter career aspirations, and no one said anything out of the ordinary until Staff Sergeant Ricardo Barraza spoke up and simply said: "Border Patrol." He told us they had special operations units and also a huge budget for training. "It's the closest thing to being an Army Ranger, but doing it in the civilian world," he said with a flourish.

Before this conversation with Staff Sergeant Barraza, I had never given a thought to what that career field looked like. All I remembered were those ugly mint-green Border Patrol trucks in the movie *Born in East L.A.,* which were just like the ones I saw as we crossed the border to vacation in Rosarito, Mexico.

I started asking more questions. What interested me most was that Staff Sergeant Barraza was Mexican. I am half Mexican on my mother's side and half Puerto Rican on my father's. I knew my mother's story and how my grandmother came across the border, but none of that registered the significance of the Border Patrol. I was ignorant regarding why any Hispanic person would ever want to protect the border from other Mexicans coming across. My initial thoughts were muddled. I wasn't considering that I was an American and currently serving our country overseas.

Barraza was explaining to me how the Special Operations teams worked and the fact they have a large budget for training, just like the Ranger Battalion. It was all sounding more attractive with every explanation he spilled. He went on to tell me that he would be applying as soon as he got out.

As my military career continued, I began teetering on whether or not I would get out or stay in. The military has a funny effect on you. You can hate most things about it, but you grow accustomed to the stability and relative comfort that it provides. Getting out was still an idea but staying in for another four years had its perks.

On December 16, 2004, I lost a close friend whom I had spent a significant amount of time with in the pipeline on the way to Ranger Battalion. Devin Peguero died while participating in a live-fire exercise. It was my first experience of losing a friend in the military. I had lost a few friends to gang violence growing up in LA, but for some reason this one hit differently. As a result, I started leaning into getting out of the military and finding a new career.

In April 2005, after returning from a deployment in Iraq,

I was preparing to be sent to Ranger School. The day before I left, we had a platoon football game: Barraza's team versus mine. Because of my competitive nature, I wanted to win so damn bad. But Barraza's competitive nature matched mine, and his team won. As I was walking off, pissed, he stopped me. "Come here," he said in his deep cocky tone. I hesitated in my frustration. "Vargas, come here," he repeated.

"What's up, Sergeant?"

He snagged a Ranger Tab off his cover, handed it to me (Rangers wear a Ranger Tab on their covers just above their rank identifier), and said: "Come back with your shit [Ranger Tab], or don't come back at all."

We hugged, and I walked off, still fuming, but also shocked by the gesture. He cut his own tab off his cover and gave it to me. This wasn't something I had ever seen anyone do. It was powerful. I didn't want to let this man down, just like I had never wanted to let my father down.

That was the last conversation I had with Staff Sergeant Ricardo Barraza. I will always regret walking away upset over a football game. I wish I had told him how much he meant to me and how much he had taught me, not only in the regiment but also in the life lessons I will take with me forever.

I was off to conquer Ranger School, and my unit was off to Iraq. If I went straight through and finished schooling, I would be able to meet them there after my graduation. I was motivated by that, and also by the fact that my projected graduation date was December 16, 2005, exactly one year to the day of Devin Peguero's death. I was motivated to get back to my platoon and to honor my friend, whose dream had been to earn his Ranger Tab.

I graduated from Ranger School right on time on December 16, and I was the Distinguished Honor Graduate. The downside was that I had severed a nerve in my shoulder during Ranger training. So, while I had hoped to rejoin my platoon overseas, the battalion physician's assistant denied my request.

Staff Sergeant Barraza was killed in Iraq from wounds he sustained on a mission. He and Sergeant Dale Brehm died while clearing a building in Ramadi, Iraq, when they came under enemy fire. We lost two of the most influential and well-respected individuals in our battalion, and I was angry about it.

Staff Sergeant Barraza's death hit me hard. Perhaps more so because I wasn't there, in-country, with him when it happened. I believed he was a better man than me. I would have gladly traded places with him. Would he have died if I had been there? Like most military men and women, I had survivor's guilt. If those bullets had hit me instead, maybe Staff Sergeant Barraza would still be alive.

When his body was flown home, I was one of the soldiers detailed to work his funeral. That was one of the hardest things I have ever had to do, but it was an honor I treasure to this day. Men like Barraza were heroes, and the fact that they were killed solidified my decision to leave the Army. I completed my last deployment to Afghanistan in 2007, and soon after that I started out-processing from active duty.

I assume that most people who decide to leave the military have some of the same motivations. You want to pursue a career where you can leverage as many of the skills you learned in the service as you can. You want to be able to provide for your family. You want to find a vocation that makes you want to get up in the morning and go to work. You want to have a job with the stability that going on multiple military deployments can't possibly give you. And for most of us—regardless of how long we serve—we are more mature and motivated at the end of our military tour of duty, and quite frankly, more confident that we are making an informed decision as to our next career choice.

I had two options in my head: firefighting or the Border Patrol. Both careers had at least a two-year path of applications, testing, and training. For peace of mind, just in case either of these options didn't work out, I applied for close to thirty jobs in the Phoenix, Arizona, area once I got out of the Army. I know it sounds odd—especially to anyone who has experienced a super-organized career track—but I didn't care that much what the job was going to be. I just wanted to feel the comfort of knowing I had a job lined up, and most importantly that I would be able to provide for my family. My father owned a rental property in Florence, Arizona, and he allowed me to live there once I got out of the military.

I applied for several fire department positions, and at one point, I was the number-one-ranked candidate for the Tucson Fire Department. The Tucson Fire Department was planning on hiring the top twenty candidates, and I was feeling good about becoming a firefighter and following the family tradition. But fate intervened, and the Tucson Fire Department went on a one-year hiring freeze, a soul-crushing turn of events. The pressure of wanting a career, not just for myself but for my family as well, weighed on me.

I was trying to build my résumé by working at a volunteer fire department in the hopes of making it harder for other fire department gatekeepers to ignore me. I decided to try to join a small, private department in Coolidge, Arizona. They had a reputation for being cowboys in the fire community. They were all young and wild dudes.

Soon after joining, I was called to fight a fire that occurred on the tour bus of a musician called Kenna. I was lead on the hose, but as I was fighting the fire, I couldn't help but feel disappointment. I had spent the last four years of my life doing some of the craziest stuff imaginable. Trying to fill that void by fighting fires wasn't working for me. It was time to focus on something else, so I shifted my focus to becoming a Border Patrol agent, for my kids, for myself, and for Staff Sergeant Barraza's memory. But this book is more than just my memoir of my time as a Border Patrol agent, it is a look behind the curtain at what the Border Patrol *is* and what it *does* to protect our nation every day.

If you are reading this book, it is because you have found yourself genuinely interested in our nation's immigration crisis and the current chaos along our southern border. It means that you, like millions of other Americans, have decided that your curiosity is no longer satisfied by bite-sized pieces of poorly sourced information, reported in scripted, biased, politically correct format

from a glossy studio in New York City. You are no longer satisfied by so-called "experts" who have never interdicted an ounce
of narcotics, never had an angry rock thrown in their direction,
and never set foot along our southern border.

You are here because you have found yourself asking questions and been unable to find satisfactory answers. This book
will provide the unvarnished truth about the reality of daily life
along the U.S.-Mexico border from the perspective of a Border
Patrol agent. The accounts and information are not only fac-
tually accurate but are validated and galvanized through lived
experience.

The very concept of a "nation" is based not only on ideals,
morals, and principles but on borders as well. Borders and
boundaries are what establish the freedom and independence of
one nation from another, and those borders must be defended.

This is the mission and ethos of the U.S. Border Patrol and
the thousands of men and women who serve in its ranks. It is
no different than the individual right to privacy and security. It
is not only why we lock our doors but why we have doors in the
first place.

The Border Patrol has been misunderstood, vilified, criti-
cized, and politicized by both supporters and detractors. It has
been compared to organizations such as the Ku Klux Klan and
even the Waffen-SS. Comparisons such as these are not only
grossly offensive and intellectually dishonest but also highly in-
accurate.

Despite this kind of ongoing criticism, the men and women
of the U.S. Border Patrol continue to do their job with honor

and integrity. They do their work mostly unseen by the American public in inhospitable and austere environments, in places like Ajo, Arizona; Eagle Pass, Texas; and Calexico, California. They continue to serve with dedication and to risk their lives every day against drug cartels, traffickers, smugglers, and a myriad of other dangers not likely experienced even by most law enforcement officers, let alone civilians.

It is important to understand the U.S. Border Patrol as it exists. It does not create immigration laws, nor does it decide immigration policies. The Border Patrol is simply the mechanism that enforces the immigration policy of each administration, and it is guided by federal law and the U.S. Constitution.

By way of analogy, bartenders do not decide the legal drinking age, and state troopers do not set the speed limit on our highways. Border Patrol agents only enforce the policies that are put into place by our nation's government. Agents are charged with defending and asserting the most fundamental right of any nation on earth: the right to defend its borders.

As you read this book, the men and women of the Border Patrol will continue to guard our borders and protect you and your loved ones without political influence, ideological contamination, or personal bias. They will enforce the laws of this nation as directed by the citizens of this country and through their elected representatives and the president.

Once I decided to begin the journey to become a Border Patrol agent, it was game on. Applying for the Border Patrol wasn't the biggest challenge—the rules and procedures were all pretty straightforward. That said, setting up the USAJobs.gov profile took me weeks. I didn't want to omit a single detail that was required to complete the application on the website.

Once you complete the application portion, you receive an email with possible test locations and dates. I was surprised by the fast turnaround. I applied for the Border Patrol and received a test date within thirty days. That was the good news. The bad news was that I feared this test more than any other part of the application process.

The written portion of the Border Patrol test was a gauntlet, and that was followed by even more hurdles: an oral exam, a physical exam, a background check, and a lie-detector test. Ultimately I passed everything with flying colors, but the process took *forever*. Finally, after two years—which I later learned was a completely normal length of time for Border Patrol admission—I was going to be hired and sent to the Academy.

But while I was celebrating my good fortune, I understood that even if I passed all these obstacles, someone—some unseen entity I had never met—would make the decision as to whether or not I would ultimately be asked to join the Border Patrol and attend the Academy. I waited and waited, but as the old saying goes, I was as nervous as a cat in a room full of rocking chairs.

Finally, the call came. I remember it like it was yesterday. The voice at the other end of the phone said: *"Mr. Vargas, congratulations, we have accepted your application, and we would like to offer you a position with the Border Patrol. Duty station will be Eagle Pass, Texas. You are scheduled to begin your training at the Border Patrol Academy on June 4; congratulations again."*

I was super stoked, and I heard my dad's voice playing in my head: "Vinny, you can't go wrong working for the government." I didn't hesitate. I said yes and thank you. But as soon as the voice on the other end clicked off, I panicked. My wife at the time was due to deliver my son Holden just days after I was to report to the Border Patrol Academy. The family came first. Do I call them back and ask for a different class date?

I was so conflicted. Here I was being invited to start the job of a lifetime, but it would mean missing one of the most important events in my life—the birth of my son. I was beating myself up, thinking that I should have spoken up before saying yes. But at the end of the day, I was committed. I was going to show up at the Border Patrol Academy and start my new career—but this was a decision I have continued to question.

I don't think I'm a worrier, but I'm a guy who likes to plan ahead and run through what might happen. This was no different. I knew one day I would have to explain to my son why I missed his birth, and hopefully he would understand that I had landed the job of a lifetime and would provide him more opportunity than I could have ever imagined. Once I had reconciled that I would be beginning my training while my son was being born, I prepared to head off to the Border Patrol Academy.

The Border Patrol Academy is where "aspirants" are transformed into "agents" who immediately man the front lines in defense of our homeland. While most of you reading this have been exposed to the training that the U.S. military receives—especially elite units like the Army Rangers or Navy SEALs—through movies, television shows, books, articles, and other media, thus far no one has peeled back the details of why the Border Patrol Academy exists, how it operates, or how, in a short time, it makes agents out of civilians.

The Border Patrol Academy provides excellent training. I say this not only as a former Border Patrol agent who has gone through it but also because the Border Patrol Academy is recognized among all law enforcement agencies—in the United States and abroad—as having one of the most challenging curriculums in federal law enforcement. All newly hired Border Patrol agents receive their foundational law enforcement skills by attending the Academy as well as other needed skills to deal with the diverse challenges Border Patrol agents will face in the field.

To give you a sense of how comprehensive this training is, each Border Patrol trainee must complete the resident courses of instruction in U.S. law, Border Patrol operations, physical training, firearms instruction, driving, law enforcement, tactical training, and Spanish. Student assessments vary from online, knowledge-based, multiple-choice exams to diverse and rigorous performance-based integrated scenarios. You have to have a huge facility to pull this off, and the Federal Law Enforcement Training Center in Artesia, New Mexico, is just that—enormous. It comprises more than thirty-five hundred acres, and it seems like every acre is dedicated to one aspect of training or another.

There is likely no other law enforcement organization in America where agents must be as well-versed in the law. It is important that you understand this, because Border Patrol agents carry a heavy burden to do the right thing, to protect the nation without trampling on the rights of those who choose to cross our borders without documentation.

A big part of this training involves understanding the myriad of legal authorities that Border Patrol agents must learn, from applied authorities, to administrative law, to a combination of natural law and immigration law. Once Border Patrol Academy students are grounded in the legal authorities that guide their actions, they move on to the Border Patrol Academy Operations program. This intense training has a heavy focus on leveraging the best technology and skill sets needed to secure our nation's borders. The curriculum includes radio and GPS operations, personal radiation detector operations, traffic checks, freight train checks, fraudulent document analysis, noncitizen processing and detention techniques, and perhaps most importantly, the tactics, techniques, and procedures to actually patrol the border.

One of the most daunting aspects of training for Border Patrol Academy students is the physical techniques curriculum. This intense program is designed to develop officer presence and increase the mental and physical capabilities of U.S. Border Patrol agents. The curriculum blends physical conditioning, defensive tactics, and less-than-lethal training to emphasize agent survival and safety and prepare trainees for the physical demands of the job. A crucial part of the curriculum for Border Patrol Academy students is the Firearms Training Department. This is a comprehensive firearms training program designed to prepare agents to act decisively within a split second to make sound and legal decisions regarding when to use or not use deadly force.

Border Patrol Academy students also undertake the U.S. Border Patrol Academy's Driver Training Department curriculum. This training is designed to prepare students with the operational driving ability, tactical skills, and occupational knowledge required to work as a law enforcement professional. Students then advance to vehicle stops, pursuit driving, controlled tire deflation devices, and offensive driving techniques. Driver training culminates with practicing vehicle stop scenarios to show students how to use a principle-based approach to resolve unconventional situations in real time.

Border Patrol Academy students undergo tactics training that incorporates both firearms and physical techniques. Tactics lessons focus on the application of law enforcement communications, critical thinking, risk management, interdictions, active threat resolution, tactical low-light operations, and basic ATV familiarization. Finally, there is Spanish-language training. This is a critical element of the job, because over 90 percent of the more than one million undocumented noncitizens apprehended each year speak only Spanish.

One important point that I want to make is that the Border Patrol Academy training is dynamic. You don't just sit in a classroom month after month. You learn enough to provide you with basic knowledge, and then you participate in what is known as scenario-based training, where instructors put you in amazingly realistic situations. For example, to teach candidates how to perform immigration checks, interview detainees, carry out drug busts, and deal with other confrontations, candidates are put into situations with Spanish-speaking actors who argue, run, or fight back. In one scenario meant to simulate a drug bust, actors playing the role of smugglers throw wads of cash at the agents-in-training, who must then decide how to act.

With that as background regarding the Border Patrol Academy as an *institution,* I now want to share *my* personal journey as an Academy student, which began before I arrived at the Federal Law Enforcement Training Center in Artesia. First I had to drive my vehicle to Del Rio, Texas, for the day one in-processing, which involved completing mountains of paperwork and other administrative chores before I could head to the Academy.

Then—and now—I felt like this was an extra step that didn't make too much sense, but I was so pumped to start the Academy that I just rolled with it. When I arrived, I pulled up to a small hotel down the street that I could tell had a big influx of other recruits who were there for the same reason. Once we all checked in to our hotel rooms, we took some time to introduce ourselves to one another. Everyone had anxiety over what was to come in the next few days. All we knew was that in the morning we would start our first day of becoming a Border Patrol agent.

I woke up early to get myself familiarized with the area. I left my hotel room about ten minutes early to slow roll my way to the sector meeting.

I immediately noticed a very big dude who was rumbling down the road. He reminded me of Bigfoot in the grainy videos I had seen. He was well dressed, with broad shoulders, a buzzed head, and gorilla-like movements. I pulled up next to him to see if he needed a ride. I wasn't trying to stereotype, but this white man in a border town stuck out like a sore thumb. He introduced himself as Chris Smilo, and I introduced myself simply as Vincent.

Chris was also in town for the same training I was, and I was curious about what he did before becoming a candidate for the Border Patrol. He told me that he had made the Minnesota Vikings as an undrafted free agent, but that he was cut from the final roster before his rookie season began. That made total sense to me, and it helped validate the fact that I was in good company. Chris became one of my best friends at the Academy because he was self-effacing and never put on airs about being so close to his dream of becoming a pro football player.

We drove to the intake portion of the hiring process, after which we were unexpectedly released for a day off before we needed to get on the bus to the Academy. Based on what they had told us about the tight restrictions we would have at the Academy, we wanted to take full advantage of that freedom. There were five of us who within two days had already become friends, and we were ready for some fun on our last full day of freedom for a while. We picked up some meat, some snacks, and some beers and headed to Lake Amistad in Amistad National Recreation Area along the Rio Grande.

After we'd had our food and beers, we decided to go for a swim. In my head, I could hear my first sergeant giving the Friday night military safety brief: "Do not drink and swim." I was reluctant, but this might be my last time hanging out before six long months of training. "Let's go!" I said.

Lake Amistad was cold as hell, but we wanted to have the

experience. Besides, I've always been a good swimmer, and the water temperature was no issue for me. Not long after we started, I realized that panic and nervousness were manifesting on Luis Alfaro's face. What the hell was going on? At first I thought he was just screwing around and faking us all out. But I was concerned, so I asked: "Are you good?"

And that's when I got *really* concerned. He couldn't answer. He was actually struggling to swim, so I turned back, grabbed him under his armpits, and dragged him all the way to the pier, where our other friends were able to pull him to safety. Alfaro admitted he was overwhelmed and out of swimming shape, which made him panic. I eventually went back and finished the swim with Smilo and another candidate.

After that "near-death" experience, we all sat around and drank some more beer and laughed it off. But there was a part of me that knew how lucky we were. If something had happened to us that day, we could have all kissed our careers goodbye. Alfaro later told me that I saved his life. I wasn't sure if the situation was really that serious and that he wouldn't have found a way to paddle to shore had I not been there, but I do know he was grateful and he became a close friend. It made me *more* comfortable entering the Academy knowing that I had already made four good friends, Chris Smilo, Luis Alfaro, Nick Soto, and Kevin Foreman who would be on this journey with me.

We finally completed all the in-processing, and we embarked on the eight-hour bus ride from Del Rio to Artesia, New Mexico. Surrounding me on my bus were about thirty men and women who, like me, had waited for two years as we powered through the Border Patrol agent application and screening process. Talk about pent-up anticipation.

When we arrived at the Federal Law Enforcement Training Center, things changed dramatically. The instructor cadre at the Border Patrol Academy conducted what we call a shark attack on the bus, boarding it like they were taking a military objective, and suddenly I was back in basic training. These instructors were decked out in hats similar to Army drill sergeants, and it was clear to all of us that they were in charge. But they weren't screaming at us at the top of their lungs—it was close to that, but not as intense.

Once they hustled us off the bus and arranged our sorry asses into something vaguely resembling a military formation, they got down to the business at hand. They explained the rank structure at the Academy, introduced themselves, and clarified who would be teaching what courses. It seemed silly to be telling us all this, as most of the candidates were so shell-shocked that they likely wouldn't remember anything that was being shouted at them.

All of this yelling was not abuse for the sake of abuse, but instead served an important purpose: to provide an introduction to operating under stress and to weed out some of those unlikely to make it through the program.

I remember standing there, trying to blend in, hoping the instructors wouldn't single me out as a former military service member and make me a class leader or something like that. I just wanted to be the gray man, blend in, get through the training, and become a Border Patrol agent. Sometimes that wasn't an easy thing to do.

I remember my first day in basic training when the drill sergeant yelled at me: "TUCK THAT CHIN IN." That was all it took, and I was no longer a gray man. Once a drill sergeant calls you out, you are forever a target. Additionally, I had two full sleeves of random tattoos that I had been hiding, which was something that was very common for the Special Operations community. I knew they would be discovered once we put on our PT gear. Also, whether I liked it or not, I just looked like a former military guy.

When we were directly told to raise our hands if we had prior military background, I raised my hand as instructed, as I did not want to risk an integrity violation. When one of the training cadre asked me about my military service, I did not volunteer much, just that I was an infantryman in the Army. Sure enough, my worst fears were realized, and the cadre pulled me to the front of the formation. They divided us into two different sections. There were sixty trainees in total, making thirty trainees in each sector. Suddenly, I was in charge of twenty-nine new friends.

Our cadre marched in its ragged formation to a building where we had to fill out more paperwork. Next, we got our uniforms, found our rooms, met our roommates, and started storing our gear. That momentary calm was broken when we marched over to meet our PT instructors. Suddenly, it was shark attack 2.0.

These instructors were super intimidating. Each one of them looked like they were in great shape and that they could out-run, out-PT, out-climb, and out-*everything* any of us. They were screaming at us like maniacs as they put us through our physical training paces. In a different life I might have been intimidated.

Since I had been "voluntold" that I was a class leader, everyone in our class came up to me for all kinds of everyday information and advice. It came down to the simplest things, everything from how to iron your pants and how to shine your boots to how to march, among dozens of other questions. It brought me back to my first days in the Army when I was the new guy asking all the questions.

After going through a number of schools in the military, I didn't have high expectations for the Border Patrol Academy. What I mean is this: The U.S. military has been around for centuries and has honed its training to be the best in the world. The Border Patrol Academy didn't have such a rich history, so I figured that the training wouldn't be on par with what I experienced in the Army.

I was pleasantly surprised. Things were super organized, and the instructors knew their stuff. I was impressed with how they moved us through classroom and physical training: When one group was in class, the other would be doing PT. Then we would switch. The classroom instructors were all specialists, and it was easy to tell that they had been teaching their specific subject for a while.

As for the PT instructors, that's a completely different story. They were in incredible shape, and I knew we had some serious sessions ahead of us. But first we had to do our intake PT. We took an initial PT test as a baseline to see if we met the Academy standards. This was important, because regardless of what kind of shape you're in when you show up at the Academy, you have to attain a certain minimum standard to graduate.

By the end of the first week, we had already lost several candidates who either had been injured due to the intensive physical training or had elected to leave due to the stress of being in a semi-military environment. This continued to happen throughout the course of the Academy training until just the last few weeks. For my class, the attrition rate was close to 40 percent. I made it through, even though I came close to failing my academic testing. Academics have never been my strong suit, and passing with an 80 percent grade came down to my final test. However, I prevailed—by the end of the Academy course of instruction, which concluded with the Spanish-language portion, I genuinely felt ready to do the job.

One important fact stands out regarding my time at the Border Patrol Academy: I felt—as we all did—that the instructor cadre did the best job anyone could to prepare us for the complex world we were about to encounter as Border Patrol agents. With my gun and badge in hand, and the skills I have picked up from the Academy, I was ready to head to my Border Patrol station at Eagle Pass, Texas, and get to work.

However, just before I left the Academy, Border Patrol Agent Robert Rosas was murdered on July 23, 2009, while performing his duties in a remote border area near Campo, California. Agent Rosas was responding to suspicious activity in an area notorious for alien and drug smuggling when he was shot and killed by unidentified assailants. This was the first line of duty death I'd experienced in my career, and I hadn't even started as an agent yet—it remains one of my most vivid memories of my time at the Academy. It was a rude awaking to the potential hazards of the job.

Reading the information of Agent Rosas's murder was chilling. He was shot and killed with his own service pistol. I imagined the struggle and fight that happened and eventually led to his murder, and it frustrated me. I hated hearing about it, but it inspired me to take my training even more seriously and challenge myself to be the best-prepared agent ever to take the field to defend our nation's borders.

2

LEARNING THE ROPES AND THE BORDER CULTURE

After graduation from the Border Patrol Academy, I drove back to Eagle Pass North Station in Del Rio Sector. Eagle Pass, Texas, borders the Mexican town of Piedras Negras, supposedly the birthplace of nachos. Who knew? I drove into town to find the new digs I had rented with a few friends.

The first thing I remember about pulling into Eagle Pass was the Mexican flag that flew on the Mexican side of the border. It was big and beautiful. It rippled in the wind and overshadowed the U.S. flag that flew at the U.S. Port of Entry (POE). It felt like a powerful message to the United States, something that instantly made my job as an agent real. It was up close and personal.

I was hungry, so I pulled into a McDonald's for a quick bite. This was when I experienced my first culture shock. The woman on the other side of the speaker asked for my order, but she did so in Spanish. Not the Spanglish I had become accustomed to growing up in a predominantly Hispanic LA neighborhood but

100 percent Spanish. I immediately felt insecure. I have always felt comfortable ordering Mexican food in Spanish. It's simple—I order the same thing every time: a chicken burrito with rice. But having to give my McDonald's order in Spanish made me uncomfortable.

This is probably a good point to explain why a Hispanic guy who was raised in a predominantly Hispanic neighborhood wasn't conversant in the Spanish language. My parents didn't teach us Spanish for fear of us struggling with speech as our oldest brother did. Sometimes when teaching a child two languages, they have trouble developing both. My brother was a late bloomer in speaking and my parents feared it was because of that issue. They felt it was best to teach us English first, assuming they would get around to Spanish later. But as the family was assimilating to California and the culture around them, the time to learn Spanish never really came about, and by the time I was in high school, it was too late.

This is a very common situation where I grew up. I imagine that all around the United States, families coming to America are trying as hard as they can to conform to their surroundings to ensure their kids are "Americanized." In LA, you're surrounded by all races, but sometimes being Hispanic and not speaking Spanish can make you a target for criticism. In some crowds you're too Hispanic, and in others you're not Hispanic enough. You can never really win.

Some would say we forgot where we came from, but I would say it's the natural progression. I personally would have benefited from knowing both languages, but hindsight is 20/20, as they say, and my parents made the best decision they could at the time.

I think you can see why the cashier's question was so damn bizarre to me. I kind of laughed at the situation and realized that this happened all the time on the border. When I was a kid and found myself in a place away from home, my mom used to say, "You aren't in Kansas anymore, Vargas," a reference to *The Wizard of Oz*. I realized then and there that I was definitely in a new world, that this was now home, and that I'd better get used to it, and fast.

I always try to arrive wherever I'm going a little early in order to get situated in the area and understand the lay of the land. Failing to prepare is preparing to fail. This was a new environment. To the untrained person, everything was a threat. I, too, was untrained in the common courtesies of border life. At first, I was cautious about everything and everyone.

My roommates, Paul Ayala and Beau Bessant (and later Miguel Tovar), and I moved into our rental house, which, unbeknownst to us, was on a street known to be swarming with drug smugglers. When this news was dropped on us, it set me a little on edge. I realized I needed to keep my head on a swivel a little more than I thought. Being that this was a new environment, I prepared for the worst. I imagined a cartel kidnapping me or putting a hit out on us because we were going to be bringing heat to the area. I thought of every possible scenario, but at the end of the day I realized that my fears were largely unfounded.

I mentioned earlier that I was married, so you are likely

wondering why I rented a place with a bunch of other dudes. Truth be told, my marriage was falling apart. It was something most people were unaware of at the time because I didn't want to talk about it much. I suspect that you can understand.

Once you arrive at your duty station, you must complete two years of training before you can be considered a Journeyman. A Journeyman is a level of competency one can reach, and the Border Patrol recognizes Journeyman status by considering that person for a permanent position. Until you reach Journeyman status, you can be released from the agency for anything that doesn't represent them in a good light. In those two years, you go through several levels of field training, which is basically what most people would call OJT—on-the-job training. You are also simultaneously participating in computer-based training and testing to ensure you are still proficient on subjects you learned at the Academy.

When I arrived at Eagle Pass North Station for morning muster, I was reunited with many friends whom I hadn't seen in three months since we trained together at the Academy. The Spanish speakers who had validated that part of the training and who had gotten their guns and badges before the rest of us were already in the field. Since I failed the Spanish proficiency test I had to stay longer. The rumor mill about me had already started, as they had been telling stories to my field training officer (FTO), Hector Sanchez.

I remember the first words Field Training Officer Sanchez used when he walked up to me. He stared at me through his thick glasses and said in a strong Spanish accent: "I heard you

were a sergeant, Mr. Vargas. Well today, I am your sergeant."
What he said didn't make any sense, and I wasn't about to correct him in military dialect. I believe he was trying to intimidate
me and assert his dominance. It was both funny and frustrating
at the same time.

Here I go again, I said to myself. *I'm twenty-seven years old
and I am starting all over. I am back to being the FNG* (fucking
new guy). FNG or not, I didn't want to do anything to stand
out; I just wanted to learn the ropes so I could do my job. I
replied, "Yes, sir!" and determined to do everything I could to
prove I was going to be an asset to and not an issue for his patrol.

The first two weeks of patrol were challenging. Our area of
responsibility was so vast and there was so much going on that
even after a few weeks I was wondering how we could successfully do our jobs. One of the most daunting challenges was the
geography. From our duty station to the farthest ranch in our
operating jurisdiction it was an easy two-and-a-half hour drive.
Additionally, that meant that roughly 140 miles of border were
covered by fewer than twenty agents per shift.

Field Training Officer Sanchez ensured that we were up to
speed with the high-tech gear we had been introduced to at the
Academy. The equipment ran the gamut from high-powered
cameras to seismic meters at the border to the newest GPS devices. Part of our indoc included nontech tools such as the old-
school cut-and-drag, which I will explain later.

I had been working "the Line" for less than a week when
things heated up. "The Line" refers to the term "Holding the
Line," a common title for the border boundary and what the job

of a Border Patrol agent entails. While our FTO was driving us back to the station to wrap up our day, we saw a group of what looked to be runners straight from the sign you see on San Diego border highways. This is a familiar sign seen on the border indicating the potential of border crossers. It is a big yellow diamond-shaped sign with silhouettes depicting a family of three. Three individuals flashed past us and hopped the short fence to try to get away.

My heart was pounding. I was confused yet excited. A huge deluge of thoughts and emotions went through my mind. *Here we go,* I said to myself. I had just landed the job I had been fighting so long to attain. I had been training for months, and now—for the first time in my new career—I was about to apprehend a group of people crossing the border illegally.

The adrenaline screamed through my veins. We jumped out of our vehicle and gave chase. We easily hopped the short fence that the runners had crossed. I teamed up with another agent and went one way, and my other two partners, who were both trainees, went another. Bad luck—I picked the wrong way. However, the other team approached the runners with so much energy that the three individuals quickly gave up.

As I walked up to support my fellow agents, I noticed that the three people apprehended were a forty-year-old male, forty-year-old female, and a female child around eight years old. I don't know why, but this moment hit me like a ton of bricks. For some reason or another, I looked at the adult female and thought of my grandmother, and I looked at the little girl and thought of my mother.

As I stood over the three illegals and helped with the field interview, the moment became bittersweet for me. I am half Mexican and half Puerto Rican. My grandmother on my mother's side was born in Chihuahua, Mexico, and crossed the border illegally when she was eighteen years old. The story that was told to me—and I believe to be true—was that her sister, Francisca, who was born in the United States and thus an American citizen, had died at a young age due to an illness. As far as my mother and I can remember, my grandmother's name was Francisca as well. To make a long story short, my grandmother stole the identity of her sister in order to become an American citizen. My mother was raised in the small town of Canutillo, Texas, near El Paso and the Mexican border.

I think that you can understand how, knowing this story about my heritage, I have always been conflicted regarding illegal immigration and border security. I am extremely proud to be an American of Mexican descent, and I will continue to uphold the same values and beliefs that my grandmother had in her desire to become an American.

But there I was, a third-generation Mexican American whose grandmother crossed into the United States illegally, who was about to apprehend some individuals doing essentially the same thing for the same reason—to have a chance at a better life. The feeling was surreal, and during my entire time as a Border Patrol agent, I wrestled with doing my duty and my empathy for the people we apprehended.

A question that every Hispanic Border Patrol agent will have to answer someday is: "Why do you turn your back on your people?" I find this to be a shortsighted question. Normally it's asked by someone of Hispanic descent who is living in America and speaking English and reaping the benefits and all the opportunities that America can provide. This person often assumes they understand the career field but misconceives its day-to-day operations. I have learned that to have any hope of initiating a meaningful discussion about border security, the first step is to help others understand that immigration policy and border security are not synonymous.

Hundreds of thousands of people risk their lives to enter this country through the canyons, deserts, and rivers along our southern border, and thousands more spend their savings to travel across the world to become students, professionals, and skilled laborers in the United States. We have to understand this is still the Land of Opportunity, and as long as that seems to fit, illegal immigration will continue to be a trending topic.

Immigration, and specifically the enforcement of immigration law, is only one subset of border security, but it's a critical one. Border security itself is much more complex, but there are ways to simplify it.

Consider border security in the context of your own personal home. Here are a few questions to frame the discussion.

- Do you care who enters your personal home? Why?
- What actions or investments do you make to ensure you can control who and what enters your personal home?

- Do you believe that you have a right to determine who enters and stays in your personal home?
- When someone comes to your home, where do you expect them to go, and what do you expect them to do?
- Do you have general time frames during which you accept visitors? Do you act differently when someone approaches your home outside of those times?
- Or you can flip the perspective: When you visit someone else, what do you do? How do you announce your arrival?

I believe that in almost every society around the world, the social norm is to present yourself at the established entry point, normally the front door. It is also a social norm to present yourself during reasonable hours and ask permission to enter.

You likely don't think about it, but every time you answer your door you do a quick threat assessment before you decide if you will even open the door, let alone allow the person to enter. Although this is a subconscious process, I guarantee you do it. Examples of thoughts that you quickly process include:

- Do you know the person or not?
- Is their behavior normal for the circumstance, or are they acting erratic?
- What are they wearing? Is it appropriate for the climate and/or surroundings?

It is commonly accepted, and in most states codified into law, that if someone attempts to enter your home without your permission, you have a right to see them as a threat and prevent their entry. Does this sound reasonable?

Homeland/border security is the same as personal home security. If you cannot control who and what enters your personal home, you have no security. If we cannot control who and what enters our homeland, we have no security, and ultimately no nation.

U.S. Border Patrol agents and U.S. Customs and Border Protection (CBP) officers are border security professionals and not simply "immigration police." In the simplest terms, CBP has the statutory mission to know and control who and what enters our national homeland. U.S. law requires everyone to come to our front door, one of 328 legally established Ports of Entry, and anyone who is not a U.S. citizen must ask permission to enter. Failure to do so is a criminal violation of 8 USC 1325. Under U.S. customs laws, even U.S. citizens are required to reenter the country through the front door, a Port of Entry, or face monetary penalties.

Within the U.S. Customs and Border Protection Agency, the Office of Field Operations has CBP officers standing by at every Port of Entry where they will meet every person seeking admittance, evaluate each item being imported, apply the immigration and customs laws that have been duly enacted by the U.S Congress, and determine what does and does not meet the established criteria for entry.

The fundamental mission of the U.S. Border Patrol has always been to detect and interdict anyone who is trying to sneak into our home without going through a Port of Entry. It really is that simple. The task is not racist, it is not xenophobic, and it is not anti-immigrant. It is the social and legal norm around the world, and it applies to everyone regardless of nationality, age, sex, or skin tone.

It is important to remove the emotions associated with immigration policy and start with the basics. I encourage you to separate the policy debates about immigration from the discussion until you accept that simply demanding that people use the front door is not unreasonable.

Despite what is typically reported in the media, the United States is one of the most immigrant-friendly and welcoming nations on earth. This not only applies to the volume and diversity of immigrants absorbed by our country every year but also to the wide variety of avenues an immigrant can take to obtain U.S. citizenship.

Before continuing, it is critical to establish certain factors to understand not only the process of obtaining U.S. citizenship but also certain terminology in order to reduce confusion. As discussed earlier, the U.S. immigration system is composed of numerous agencies operating under various legal doctrines to provide specific, but varied, services to the public. For the purposes of this explanation, the simplest approach is to divide the agencies into enforcement agencies and administrative agencies.

Law and immigration enforcement agencies operate in the United States to ensure that legal immigration and trade are facilitated, illegal immigration is prevented and mitigated at the border, and immigration enforcement takes place inside the

United States. These agencies include Customs and Border Protection (Border Patrol, Air and Marine, Office of Field Operations) and Immigration and Customs Enforcement (ICE). Think of these agencies as the security personnel outside a concert arena or any other large venue. They are responsible for checking tickets, preventing weapons and other prohibited items from being smuggled in, generally ensuring that everyone behaves, and in some cases, removing people who have either circumvented the entry points and snuck in or violated some rule after being admitted. The enforcement agencies of our immigration system function in a similar fashion. They are responsible for protecting the physical borders of the United States and ensuring that anyone entering this country is properly identified and screened.

The administrative agencies, on the other hand, establish policies in accordance with immigration law and maintain a fair and equitable system for awarding, issuing, and processing visa requests. They are also responsible for processing other immigrant benefit claims such as adjustments of status and naturalization petitions. These agencies would be the equivalent of a venue and ticket issuing company.

Before discussing and defining immigration, it is important to understand the concept of citizenship. In the United Sates there are two basic paths by which a person can obtain citizenship: *birth* or *naturalization.* First, you can be born inside the United States or any of its legal territories and automatically become a citizen. This concept is referred to as "jus soli," a Latin phrase that translates to "right of soil." Jus soli, commonly referred to as "birthright citizenship," is the right of anyone born in the territory of a state to nationality or citizenship and is the most straightforward of the two paths to citizenship. However, citizenship by birth also includes *derived citizenship* or *transferred citizenship* from parents. For example, a child born to two U.S. citizens who are on vacation in France would still derive U.S. citizenship.

The second path to citizenship is naturalization, a course of action that allows people to immigrate to the United States and become citizens. It also allows for anyone in the United States with a legal immigration status to petition for relatives living abroad to immigrate as well. This has been referred to as "chain migration," and it is the most common way for those not lucky enough to have won the geographic birth lottery to become U.S. residents and citizens. This principle of sponsorship applies in the same way that a current member of a private club could sponsor a nonmember for status and membership.

Now that we have defined the concepts guiding the acquisition of citizenship, it is important to discuss and clarify the most confused and misused element in the entire debate around immigration—the term itself. Simply put, immigration is the transition of people from one country to another. This transition can either be temporary or permanent, and it can occur either legally or illegally.

Legal immigration takes place through a formal request by a non–U.S. resident or citizen living in another country asking permission to enter the United States. This process is done through U.S. embassies and consulates abroad and allows the U.S. government to properly vet and clear anyone attempting to visit or live in the United States.

Illegal immigration is the intentional circumvention of this legal immigration process where people either enter the United States between the official Ports of Entry without being vetted or arrive in the United States legally but under false pretenses. The most common example of the first type of illegal immigration would be an individual crossing the Rio Grande river along the southern border and being picked up and transported to the interior of the country. The most common example of the second type would be someone arriving on a tourist visa with the intention of living and working in the United States permanently. Again, legal immigration is like being invited into one's home—that invitation must be extended to the guest by the homeowner. Anyone arriving without an invitation and prior approval would be considered an intruder at worst and an inconvenience at best. Before inviting anyone into your home, you would also like to know how long they intend to stay. Obvious preparations and considerations must be made when considering if a guest will stay for several hours to enjoy dinner and drinks, sleep on your couch for a few nights while their home is being renovated, or move into your basement and live with you and your family for the rest of their life.

The term *immigrant* applies to anyone who intends to abandon residency in their native country and permanently immigrate to the United States. Immigrant visas can be issued to anyone who is related to and is being sponsored by a U.S. citizen or permanent resident, someone who is married or engaged to be married to a U.S. citizen or resident, or someone who is seeking employment in the United States.

The term *nonimmigrant* applies to any individual who intends to enter the United States on a temporary basis. Although there are over two dozen categories of nonimmigrant visas, the most common are tourist visas, work visas, exchange program visas, NAFTA trade visas, and student visas. The holders of such visas are visitors who do not intend to live in the United States permanently, and are therefore not seeking citizenship.

Although the process of attaining citizenship may appear to be convoluted and less than streamlined, the actual steps are simple. First, an individual must legally enter the United States as either an "intending immigrant" or, in some cases, a nonimmigrant who will later adjust their status. Second, they must become a permanent resident and live in the United States.

Residency requirements vary in certain cases, but as a rule, one must live in the United States for five years. Finally, after meeting the five-year requirement the immigrant can submit an application for naturalization. When it comes to eligibility for U.S. citizenship, the most common paths are being related to a U.S. citizen, marrying a current U.S. citizen, serving in the U.S. military, or being a lawful permanent resident "green card" holder for a period of five years.

As my time at Eagle Pass continued under the tutelage of Field Training Officer Sanchez, the full impact of my career choice started to sink in. Wearing the uniform of the U.S. Border Patrol was one of the highlights of my life. There is something incredibly ennobling about standing at the edge of your country and protecting its 330 million citizens. Border Patrol agents are the last line of defense against those who would penetrate our border illegally.

There is something else, too, that attracted me to the Border Patrol. There is a saying many military people have voiced in the past that remains true today: Military service consists of hours of boredom punctuated by moments of terror. Terror comes in many forms, whether it is the uncertainty a Navy fighter pilot feels while trying to land a Navy jet on an aircraft carrier during a black-ass night, the tension an Army infantryman suffers while on a night mission to search for a terrorist, or the panic a Special Operations rookie tries to keep at bay while making his first parachute jump. Terror can be part of any military operation.

Border Patrol agents can experience this long boredom on a day-to-day basis, and the moments of terror arrive quickly and unexpectedly. We must be ready for virtually any event to happen at any moment. We work the areas where we are assigned, performing routine line operations, and then in a split second we are giving chase to traffickers or drug smugglers.

My point is this: Just like professional athletes put on their game face right before a match, it is "game on" every day and every night for Border Patrol agents. You have to always bring your A game, and you can never phone it in.

As with any profession—especially law enforcement—the Border Patrol has its own culture, which is further broken out into subcultures depending on where the agent serves along the southern border that stretches from California to Texas. To help you *really* understand what goes on day-to-day in the life of a Border Patrol agent, you have to understand this culture.

Border Patrol culture is ingrained during the time agents are socialized into their profession and taught how to get things done. A less fancy way of saying this is that culture is learning the ropes. It should come as no surprise that when the Customs and Border Protection leadership drafts rules and regulations for how Border Patrol agents are to perform their duties, that direction must trickle all the way down to the agents on the ground. Some of it makes it all the way down untouched, and some is tweaked a bit. Culture is learning the ropes.

To help explain what I mean by culture, I want to cycle back to something that every Army private hears from his or her sergeant: "There's the right way, the wrong way, and the Army way." This is likely the case in all organizations: You go through a great deal of training, but once you show up in your first unit, you really learn what your job entails—you learn the ropes.

Each time I learned the ropes of an organization or unit, I was able to incorporate what I learned into my socialization, and it became one aspect of the culture I passed along to rookies once I moved up in the ranks. I'm nearly certain that all new Border Patrol agents experienced this same indoctrination once they joined their first unit.

I wanted to put together a list of items that I became aware of while settling into my job as an agent. This list should better explain the culture of the Border Patrol while working in the field.

ONE IS NONE AND TWO IS ONE: This is the rule we go by when packing our gear for the field. It something we live by as agents when we are on patrol. I had learned a lot in the military, but this was the first time I had ever heard this term, and it meant a lot in this field of work. I spent plenty of time training soldiers and prepping gear in the military. In the military new recruits tend to pack more than they need, but once they have dismounted their share of vehicles and helicopters and cleared their share of buildings, they start to streamline their gear so it is efficient yet functional. This is no different in the Border Patrol. One is none and two is one means that if you have one flashlight, then you have none. If that flashlight goes out while you are chasing a group of people, you are screwed. In my tricky bag I have two and sometimes three of everything, including batteries, flashlights, tourniquets, ammo, and just about everything else I can think of. More on this tricky bag in a bit.

THE TERRAIN: The terrain we patrol is unforgiving. It's a death-trap desert in the summer and a bitterly cold moonscape in the winter. The duty areas can be five minutes from the station, but sometimes they can be an hour away from anything. There are some cacti that can go straight through the thickest boots. The bushes have fingers waiting to pluck out that extra piece of gear you don't have tightened down enough. Again, one is none and two is one.

THE COMMUNITY: Who lives on the border? Some inhabitants, including families, have lived in the area for many years, but there are others who I like to call imports that are newer: federal agents, oil field workers, and drug traffickers. Some of these career fields can be of dual purpose, meaning that it is not uncommon for an oil rigger or a politician to become a part-time drug smuggler. Nothing is unheard of in a border town. At night there are a limited amount of hangout locations so it was not absolutely uncommon to be at the bar knowing that the people across the room could be drug smugglers by day and drinkers at night. During the day it's a cat-and-mouse game trying to deter drugs and smuggling, but at night we refueled for what was to come the next day.

The community can be the most interesting collection of people. The honest truth about border towns amid an ongoing war on drugs and trafficking is that corruption is potentially everywhere: It can manifest in a native of the town, a politician, and even a law enforcement official. There are the righteous, and then there are the ones who fall victim to corruption.

CUTTING SIGN: This is the main skill set of being a Border Patrol agent: tracking. The term "sign" comes from the imprint that is left when someone or something has disrupted the terrain. The sign indicates that an object, animal, or human has created the disturbance. Cutting sign is an art and a highly valued skill set that can make or break an agent's career. Finding a footprint in the soft dirt is one thing, but identifying turned-over rocks on asphalt is something very few can do. There are some elite agents who can track on the run. Those are always the guys on shift you call when you have a large group in difficult terrain.

THE TRICKY BAG: Also known as the duty bag, it contains everything an agent may need in the field. A good tricky bag is an absolute essential if you want to have a good career as a Border Patrol agent. Think of the Boy Scouts motto: "Be prepared." The tricky bag almost always has these items in it: two or more flashlights, a cutting light for cutting sign at night (you must find the right angle to see the shadows and this light is essential), extra batteries for everything, your duty radio, ammo, extra pistol magazines, a medical kit, water, lunch, a hydration pack, and anything extra you think you might need in the middle of nowhere.

I also carried a slingshot in mine, something I picked up on a mission in Iraq. Sergeant Barraza of Ranger Battalion once mentioned that lights can sometimes mess with your night vision, which what gave us the advantage during an operation. On one patrol, when we were clearing a city block looking for a high-value target (a known terrorist connected to car bombs that were killing innocent people in Baghdad), we exited a house and positioned ourselves to enter the courtyard of the next, but the house's light was blinding our vision. I said that I could throw a rock and try to knock out the light. In that moment between chaos and comedy we laughed and shrugged our shoulders, and I threw the rock. My first release I was way off, but my background in college baseball hadn't left me entirely, and I was able to throw one last strike. Pow! The light shattered, and we stormed the house giggling like little kids. In the hooch afterward, we talked about other options in the event this happened again. Some guys started carrying BB guns to get dogs to leave the area. I started carrying a slingshot because it was less stressful on my arm and more accurate in a pinch. Finally, my tricky bag had VS-17 Panel. This is a high-visibility panel used by the U.S. military that allows someone on the ground to be properly identified by adjacent units as well as overhead aircraft and GPS. It was something I used many times in the Border Patrol to gain the attention of air assets trying to locate me on the ground.

BUDDY SYSTEM: Being a Border Patrol agent means you have entered a buddy system career field. The concept is similar to what Navy and Air Force pilots learn from day one: Never leave your wingman. When you come upon tracks, you call it in, and the next closest agent responds to help. At any given point, you could have half the unit working that sign if enough agents are called in. This is not the profession for the macho loner who thinks he or she can take on the world solo.

LANDMARKS: Landmarks are terms, or slang, that have been passed down by Border Patrol agents from one generation to the next. Throughout a given sector, there are landmarks that only the Border Patrol agents in that sector would know. Some of these landmarks are as basic as "the burnt house," which could refer to an old, burned-down house that was never rebuilt. "The Christmas tree" could be a gas tank in the middle of an orchard that looks like a Christmas tree on the cameras at night. These are quick references that can direct agents to areas where other agents need assistance or to send an agent to align the path of travel of a group of illegal immigrants trying to gain entry to the United States so that other agents can try to cut them off.

GROUP: This term is used in reference to multiple illegal immigrants that have been identified via foot signs or cameras. Perhaps the group is simply immigrants making an illegal entry into the United States, or maybe it's two or more drug smugglers. Agents work together to track them down, using several techniques to catch up to the group. Basic sign cutting and a GPS help create a solid direction to cut them off before getting to a main road where they might escape in a vehicle.

GPS: GPS is just as important as a gun and flashlight in the field. We work as a team, and knowing how to plug in the correct number to pinpoint a partner when he or she has apprehended someone, or is in chase deep into a hundred-acre ranch, is crucial not only to our success but also to our safety and survival. Ensuring that our partners know how to find us is as basic as blocking and tackling in football.

Another part of the culture of the Border Patrol is that almost every agent I have met has been a patriot. Without getting too misty-eyed about it, *that* was perhaps the most important part of our culture. It meant guarding our border, while at the same time treating people crossing the border, many just looking for a better life or escaping violence in their home country, with dignity and compassion.

I firmly believe this isn't something you can teach in a classroom or learn from reading an instruction manual. You have to *live it* while holding the line and absorbing the wisdom of the senior agents you are working with. The good news is that Border Patrol agents make a career out of it, unlike many in the military who just do one enlistment and get out. The average age of a Border Patrol agent is forty years old. Our profession continues to benefit from that experience. It helps rookie agents get over the culture shock they encounter on day one, and it helps them *learn the ropes.*

I've provided you with a number of definitions and other information. Now it's time to take you on a "ride-along" so you can understand what we actually *do* as Border Patrol agents. In the previous chapter, I shared how our culture and socialization happen and especially how we learn the ropes—how *I* learned the ropes. It is difficult to explain, but at some point you finally feel, to borrow an aviation term, that you are "safe for solo."

To emphasize, the sheer variety of what you can encounter on any given day working as a Border Patrol agent is breathtaking. It can include routine patrol operations (colloquially known as line watch), tracking and hunting smugglers, capturing and processing large groups of undocumented persons, participating in car chases to apprehend fleeing suspects, and much more. The point is that while "holding the line" might sound like something static, every day is dynamic.

Earlier I made the point that the Border Patrol only has a discrete number of agents who must patrol vast stretches of the southern border. For any of you who have served in the military and stood "watch," I suspect that you understand that what might seem like a big number of agents is actually much less. But let me explain further.

Guarding our border occurs around the clock. This means that in a twenty-four-hour day there are three watch shifts. Currently there are approximately twenty thousand Border Patrol agents, but when you take into consideration agents who are on leave, in training, sick, or not available for other reasons, you have to divide that number by four. Clearly, this makes maintaining an appropriate number of active agents in the field more challenging. One of the most important things we do every day is to "cut and drag" an area and report whether or not there are humans trying to cross the border in that defined space. This takes time, and it takes manpower.

Across most of the Eagle Pass border, and I believe most of the southern border, there are specific dirt roads that the Border Patrol "cuts." Cutting sign on these roads entails nothing more than driving really slowly and observing any disturbances. This isn't a secret. All trafficking organizations know this and do everything they can to avoid those roads. When you arrive at your AO (area of operations), you do an initial cut to see if there has been any traffic. Sometimes the traffic is the local population doing their day-to-day routine. But sometimes you come across "fresh" sign that suggests a group moving north. This is why having a partner is essential. A group could mean *many* people. And many people could mean a potentially risky apprehension.

Over the next few months, FTO Sanchez took us to every well-known route for trafficking and smuggling. He did this to give us the upper hand in our careers. These are high-traffic areas that have been consistently used for dope smuggling or for persons attempting to enter illegally. He was also very adamant about making sure we knew every location of sensors and cameras so we could use them to assist our units when that time came.

I had a mission to become the best Border Patrol agent I could be, and had hopes to eventually make it through the selection process for the Border Patrol Special Operations teams. I was doing everything in my power to achieve these goals without hitting any speed bumps. While he had been a mentor earlier, things were beginning to change. FTO Sanchez was starting to feel like a speed bump. I had the feeling he expected a lot out of me and that's why he would continue to challenge me on everything we did. It felt part initiation and part intimidation. I experienced this before in the military and was trying to find the patience to manage it along with the rest of the stress of being the new guy.

Therefore, on the day FTO Sanchez challenged me to a push-up contest, I didn't smoke him. I played nice. I barely beat him so he could keep his pride and not feel embarrassed around the other trainees. Years ago I read a book called *The 48 Laws of Power,* and it discussed ways to communicate with someone who is in a superior position. One should never fully take away the power of a superior or they could see you as a threat. I didn't want him to feel threatened by me; I was only trying to get out of the field-training portion of the journey so I could get to my actual unit and start doing my job.

During one of our day shifts, we were holding the line, doing our regular duties, working with FTO Sanchez. Before we headed to our units fully trained and full time, we came across some abandoned dope bundles. I had heard about them, but I had never actually seen one in person. They are the most talked about things in the Border Patrol.

Seizing dope is the most dangerous mission for Border Patrol agents because it has the potential to lead to violent engagements. The bundles average between eighty and one hundred pounds and are generally carried by hundred-pound juveniles. The dope smugglers do this because young people cannot be prosecuted as adults, and in most cases they get a slap on the wrist and a ride back to the Mexican side of the border.

We had one last important training event. Before we were released to our units full time, FTO Sanchez had us work the night shift to better understand the nuances of night traffic. I was excited to get this block of instruction out of the way and get to my unit to do my job as a fully ready Border Patrol agent.

We worked with the current unit on the ground, available to assist them in their efforts but basically just to observe. There was a group the unit was tracking, and we were all looking to come across their sign. In the midst of this operation, the camera tower called and mentioned they had eyes on a group of four people coming across the river, and gave us the landmark of just under a train bridge. This was a common route traveled in the Eagle Pass, Texas, area of operations. There was a train that went into Mexico and illegal traffic would use that as a landmark for crossing the river near a heavily populated area that would give them the highest probability of getting lost in the chaos of the urban environment.

I remembered the landmark and knew we were pretty close to the area. We were close enough that I could jog over and try to assist. I asked FTO Sanchez if I could get one other guy and go over there to help. He looked around and gave me trainee John Porter. We were off and running.

John Porter and I attended the Academy together. Truth

be told, he was an odd duck. Every time I looked at him, he appeared to be sleeping. Overall, he was a sloppy mess. Can you imagine how stressed and conflicted I felt on my first real mission? And what the hell was FTO Sanchez thinking when he gave me Porter as a partner? Now there I was, about to try and catch my first group of illegal border crossers with the support of Porter. Would he help me, or would he be a liability in this nighttime chase?

We jogged to the train bridge, where cameras helped guide us in on the last known location of the individuals we were chasing. The Eagle Pass/Mexico border is covered in cane agricultural growth—a plant that looks similar to sugar cane. I believe it was initially planted to help slow the erosion of the land around the Rio Grande river. Either way, it is extremely dry and cracks when you walk on it. That gave us a huge advantage, as we could lie in wait at a place where we were pretty sure they would cross, and we knew that they would have to make some amount of noise when they tried to break through the cane.

Suddenly, I could hear the unmistakable sound of cane breaking. It sounded like a bull was crashing through it, and the level of noise suggested a large group was coming through. Now it was game on, and our target was within reach. Our level of tension and stress jacked up to an unbelievable level.

I made a game plan with Porter. I wanted to let the group we were trying to apprehend cross the drag road before we tried to approach. That seemed to be a safe bet since we had night vision and they likely didn't. It would allow us to observe their hands and determine the threat level. I told Porter to move across the street and wait for my signal. I asked if he remembered his hand signals from the military. He nodded yes. Still, I was concerned about what Porter would do once we jumped this group.

Porter got himself into position and his demeanor changed completely. He was in a tactical crouch, eyes squinted, looking for the people we were chasing and waiting for them to break through the cane so we could get eyes on. He looked at me and signaled "five walking," with his fingers, creating a walking motion.

Roger got it, I said to myself. Suddenly, he held his hand up in a fist signaling for me to freeze. He tucked himself into the shadows a little more, and we observed them crossing the drag road.

There they were! I counted: one . . . two . . . three . . . four . . . five as they tiptoed across the drag. The feeling was indescribable. Porter and I looked at each other and we both gave a head nod. I yelled, *"Parate!"* (a Spanish colloquialism for stop).

They ran! We yelled at them again as we began the chase. We identified ourselves as federal agents. They ran through the next growth of cane and then stopped and took a knee and gave up. I am sure it was terrifying to be surprised at night by agents charging in on them, but I was even more surprised that they stopped and didn't scatter. At least some of them would likely have gotten away.

I made the call on the radio and our backup support came within minutes. We had finally experienced what it was like to apprehend individuals crossing our border illegally. I have to admit that it was a rush, and like many things in life, the first time you do something is typically the most memorable.

I have to say one last word about Agent Porter. Although at first he seemed to be more of a threat than an asset, I was sorely mistaken. I truly feel that he was struggling with PTSD from his time in Iraq throughout the Academy and the FTO portion of the training process. You hear stories of men and women who "turn on" in a moment of stress. Porter was everything I wanted in a partner, and I would have been comfortable working a group entering the country illegally with that combat-experienced medic as my partner anytime.

We detained the group, read them their rights, and began to head to the station, but as they say, "The job's not over until the paperwork is done." I learned to hate this part of the job. Processing paperwork is the most tedious thing we do as Border Patrol agents, but it is a necessary evil.

Although this was a good example of what Border Patrol agents' jobs entail in apprehending people trying to cross the border illegally, few people understand what happens once we have that person in custody. This is an important thing to explain in some detail. Processing those who cross our border illegally is the most important part of the job. Everyone and everything that we apprehend must be processed through a complex system that collects and stores information related to the incident, such as geolocation of the apprehension or discovery. It includes fingerprinting those who have been apprehended, identifying their country of origin, and other detailed information. By the time this first step of processing is complete, we have a comprehensive dossier on each individual, whether we are dealing with illegal immigration, drugs, or juvenile deportation.

What most don't understand about this process is that once the Border Patrol apprehends the individuals crossing the border illegally and completes the processing they're responsible for, they turn them over to Immigration and Customs Enforcement (ICE), which conducts further processing before transporting them to holding facilities until an immigration judge can make a determination in their case.

Let me repeat: The Border Patrol's main job is to apprehend persons who cross our borders illegally, while ICE is responsible for everything else that happens to that person until he or she is allowed to stay in the United States or is deported to their country of origin. ICE houses these illegal immigrants in holding facilities, sometimes for months on end, as immigration judges have overwhelming caseloads. In the majority of cases, those holding facilities are jails.

Immigration judges are typically backed up for about six months or more. During this time of holding, the apprehended persons will receive food, medical treatment, and housing while they await their hearing. Depending on the area of illegal crossing, the immigration judge can make a determination of deportation or a longer jail sentence. Sometimes during this process, a judge can allow entry into the country if the court can find evidence of the need for political asylum due to country-of-origin hardships.

3

THE "PROCESS"

Few Americans have even a basic understanding of just what happens to undocumented immigrants once they are apprehended at the southern border. Therefore, I want to continue what I shared in the last chapter regarding that "process" and explain the strengths and weaknesses of the current system. Additionally, it is worth mentioning that this process is somewhat different depending on the state. This means that Border Patrol agents must adapt their methods and actions depending on where they are assigned.

As I mentioned in the previous chapter—but it bears repeating—undocumented migrants' rights are scrupulously protected by Border Patrol agents. The "packet" we develop for each person is designed to ensure that when they enter the system after they are handed over to the U.S. Immigration and Customs Enforcement service, they are afforded the human rights every person—regardless of status—deserves.

What follows is the nuts-and-bolts explanation of what happens on the ground where I worked, not what a textbook might say. When someone is brought to the Border Patrol station for processing, agents must first determine who they are; whether they have any wants or warrants in this country, or any other country; and whether they are traveling as an individual or as part of a family unit.

Despite what is often reported in the news about the immigration process, little is known or understood about the complex labyrinth of our immigration system and the many overlapping, and sometimes contradictory, roles of the various agencies involved in the apprehension, detention, and adjudication of the millions of people who enter the United States illegally each year. To better contextualize this system, consider what you know about the healthcare system. Although on the surface people may use terms like "the hospital" or "healthcare" when describing the application of medical treatment or the prescription of drugs, the reality is that there are many layers and compartments to this vast network. From the administrative side of any hospital to the medical staff and the support staff, as well as the insurance companies that oversee the financial aspects of the care network, each entity has its own roles and responsibilities.

The immigration system is just as vast and complicated, sometimes even more so. People often misappropriate terminology like "immigration" or "deportation" without understanding which agency is conducting the work they are describing. Therefore, it is important to understand the role of the U.S. Border Patrol within the greater system. Although most people understand the enforcement role of the Border Patrol, few understand or even acknowledge that the USBP plays a limited role in detention and removal.

Once the apprehension takes place in the field and the people are officially in custody, the laborious and bureaucratic immigration process downshifts into the lower gears of determining citizenship and identity, conducting record checks, doing interviews, determining credible fear and asylum claims, finding family, and allocating temporary housing and overnight bed space.

This procedure is what the Border Patrol refers to as *processing*.

While the art of tracking and the tactics of interdiction make a Border Patrol agent part wild land guide/tracker and part rural police officer, *processing* turns the same Border Patrol agent into a humanitarian, a social worker, a grief counselor, an asylum interviewer, and a first-aid medical technician. Agents have done everything from consoling grief-stricken family members who lost a loved one hours earlier while crossing the border to delivering babies on the floor of a holding cell and providing lifesaving critical care for the gravest of life-threatening injuries and health conditions. In fact, it is this dual-purpose mission of the Border Patrol that was the main catalyst for the creation of BORSTAR.

Despite what is commonly believed about the way migrants are treated when they are in custody, the agents I have worked with over the years have demonstrated compassion and empathy when dealing with those who were put in their care. Even though the Border Patrol is not designed or authorized for long-term detention, every Border Patrol facility does what it can to accommodate those in their care and custody and to minimize suffering and discomfort while maximizing safety and empathy.

In fact, this ethos is taught at the Border Patrol Academy to new agents as a standard to uphold.

Processing begins in the field by the very agents who conduct the apprehension. Everyone who is apprehended is given a cursory evaluation to determine risk, both to the agents and the others in their group, and vulnerability. The persons being taken into custody are evaluated to ensure that no life-threatening injuries have been sustained during the arrest and that everyone is safe, unarmed, and compliant.

Vulnerable individuals are also identified and, in some cases, separated from the rest of the group. This includes single females and small children traveling alone. Dangerous subjects are also "flagged" and routinely separated from the group. This is done to ensure that a guide or smuggler apprehended with the group does not have a chance to intimidate or threaten the members of the group into not cooperating with the agents during processing.

The next step is to identify each member of the apprehended group and conduct a thorough record check to ensure that no one is wanted for a serious crime, or is listed or reported missing or the victim of a crime. Border Patrol agents have routinely identified missing and exploited children as well as countless fugitives wanted for rape, murder, and other violent crimes. Although most people encountered by Border Patrol carry some sort of identification, a fingerprint check and several database checks are conducted prior to any formal processing that takes place.

Once identity is established, agents determine the nationality of the individual. Many encounters are often second, third, or even fourth arrests, and many of the people attempting to enter the United States illegally have done so before, both successfully and unsuccessfully. Although most individuals travel with their country's passport or identification documents, some are actively trying to conceal their true nationality in order to be deported to Mexico rather than being sent further into the interior of Central or South America.

Given simple geographic considerations, it is to the subject's advantage to return to Mexico rather than be removed to Guatemala or El Salvador, let alone to Pakistan or Bangladesh, and repeat the entire dangerous and costly journey again. Given this motivation, it is not surprising that many people elect to lie about their nationality. And the Border Patrol must determine what is true based on some rudimentary yet ingenious elicitation techniques.

Before further exploring the processing techniques used to identify and classify each person taken into custody, it is critical to understand the logistics and motivational factors of the smuggling process from the smuggler's perspective. The logistics of any smuggling network are no different from those of a legitimate parcel service or travel arrangement organization.

The formula is simple:

Passenger + Distance + Risk = Price

The sad reality is that human smuggling is, at its core, a business, and an extremely lucrative one. Although categorizing people during the immigration screening process based on ethnicity, race, and national origin has been demonized by the

Western media and the elites of our most powerful institutions as an unnecessary and racist practice, this classification system was developed and deployed by the organizations actually perpetrating the human trafficking, not the U.S. immigration authorities.

The true origins of this system are based on the prices being charged by the smuggling organizations exploiting and abusing the people they extort, rob, rape, and sometimes murder, and not the immigration and border security professionals left to care for and protect these vulnerable people.

The smugglers typically break down their human cargo into one of three groups: Mexican, Other Than Mexican (OTM), and Exotic.

As the name implies, a *Mexican* is any person who is a Mexican national traveling to the United States to be reunited with family or an economic migrant looking for financial opportunities. Although true statistics are difficult to pinpoint due to the ever-evolving nature of the current border crisis, this group has traditionally made up as much as 90 percent of all apprehensions along the southern border.

The designation *Other Than Mexican (OTM)* classifies any person traveling from a country other than Mexico. Although this term could be applied to a citizen or national of literally any other country on earth, this moniker is traditionally used for individuals from other Latin American nations such as El Salvador, Honduras, and Guatemala.

The *Exotic* category considers anyone from places like Asia, the Middle East, or Europe. For these individuals to get from country of origin to their end destination, it takes extensive planning and logistical consideration. These lesser-known and much-less-publicized cases are often the most indicative of the larger issue of our border insecurity. Over the last twenty years the Border Patrol has apprehend thousands of exotic and special interest aliens attempting to enter the United States, including active members of the Russian Mafia and people from other Eastern European crime syndicates with active ties to terrorist organizations such as ISIS and Al-Qaeda.

The passenger will often be the most important determining factor for both the destination and risk. A subject from Egypt may be looking to travel to California to be reunited with his family, while a member of the Mexican Mafia may be attempting to travel from Mexico to Chicago after being deported by ICE only weeks prior. The distance of travel is therefore used to calculate what the smuggler charges. For the purposes of what I am sharing, the reductive format is simply that: *The further one is traveling, the more of a price they have paid.*

The risk is typically a combination of the first two factors (passenger and distance) but is usually coupled with additional circumstances such as route of travel, likelihood of apprehension, consequence of apprehension, profile and identity of the passenger, and other factors. The risk can be any issue the smuggler anticipates, which they can use to inflate the price for transporting and concealing the individual.

Apply this formula to yourself and think, *What would it take for me to do this?* You can further apply this to any hypothetical crime for a demonstration of how and why this risk-versus-reward analysis drives smuggling prices ever higher. Imagine the considerations that go into planning a crime. What will be gained versus what will be risked? And the risk doesn't stop as soon as the crime has been committed—you risk detection and apprehension long after you have successfully completed the act. Despite most humans' self-validated belief that they are good and law-abiding people, it is this primary and primal fear of consequence that guides our decision-making algorithm and keeps us from committing murder every time we experience a bout of road rage.

Most people self-restrain after weighing the consequences and long-term loss versus short-term gain. It is these same principles that guide the behavior of any criminal organization. The risk must be worth the reward. Being apprehended with a van full of Egyptian nationals in Salt Lake City, Utah, is much riskier than walking a few Mexicans from Sonora, Mexico, to Nogales, Arizona.

Despite what is commonly believed, most people being brought into the United States are willing participants in the process. This is the dramatic distinction between *trafficking* and *smuggling*. Different states have employed different tactics in discouraging illegal crossings in their respective areas, and this has also guided the behavior of those attempting to enter the United States.

Just as physical barriers such as border walls, canyons, mountains, and inhospitable terrain prevent many people from attempting to enter at a specific point, the legal consequences—automatic jail time in many cases—prevent many areas from being particularly popular for crossings. Antithetically, jurisdictions with more accommodating and relaxed rules have seen a dramatic rise in illegal entries and apprehensions due to a permissive political climate and a lax enforcement posture.

Thus, the reluctance to be apprehended is shared by both the smuggler and the individual paying to be smuggled. If any subject who is being smuggled is apprehended, the goal becomes minimization and deception. The smuggler will often attempt to conceal his role and pretend to be one of the migrants in the group—although this is typically easy for a well-trained agent to determine—and some sophisticated tactics have surfaced in various sectors for agents to assist them in these efforts.

To protect the integrity of current and future operations, I will not discuss the methods and procedures the Border Patrol uses to determine which individual is the guide or smuggler in the group. But know that USBP agents are skilled at observation, both in the field and in the processing room.

Verifying the identity of the people being smuggled or entering in a group can be difficult at times. Agents conduct simple yet sophisticated interviews to determine nationality. Questions are asked of each subject being processed to determine their national origin. As previously noted, many people from countries other than Mexico will often claim to be Mexican to be returned there instead of their own country, any of which is farther away from the U.S. border. In much the same way that you would determine if someone were indeed from your home state is the way many agents determine whether someone is in fact from Mexico. Asking questions about local culture, politics, geography, and history are often simple methods to determine national identity.

Thus far, I've spoken in "macro" terms regarding the Border Patrol in general. Now I want to focus on the "micro" and relate a specific event that happened in December 2011. I tell you this story to emphasize that Border Patrol agents must either come to the job with the ability—or they must quickly learn how—to treat every person apprehended with compassion and empathy.

There was a photo being sent around the sector, an image of a little girl that looked no older than ten handing a note to a kneeling Border Patrol agent in the early morning fog. The location was familiar. It was an orchard that divided the Eagle Pass stations. Without knowing the context of the photo, I could see that it depicted the emotional and sadly honest reality of what we encounter daily. I was so touched by the image—I wanted to know more about this little girl and her backstory. I texted my roommate, Beau, and asked who the agent in the picture was and what was the deal.

It turned out that the story was so incredible I had to add the firsthand account to this book. Here are the written records of the Border Patrol agent in the photo.

It was a cold and foggy December morning about a week before Christmas. I was working day shift which was from 0600 to 1400. My assignment for that day was the Leonard's orchards located right behind the station. I got to my area as usual and parked on loop 480 which skirts the orchard. Where I was parked, I had positioned myself to have a good visual of the orchard and the loop.

About an hour into my shift, I noticed what appeared to be the outline of a figure in the fog in between the orchard and the loop. From the loop, I thought the figure could have been an adult, just one at a far distance. As the figure got closer and began to emerge from the fog, I noticed that it was not an adult, but a little girl. I called to the child in Spanish and she began to walk toward me.

There I stood, while this little girl who was no more than ten years old cried and explained how she was lost. She was wet, cold and scared. I knelt down to be eye-level with her so that I could calm her down and reassure her that everything was going to be okay. I spoke to her like I would speak to my own daughter who was about the same age.

I flipped the switch from Border Patrol Agent to father. I began by asking her if she was all right and also asked her where her parents were. She responded as a scared child would, with a high pitched and crackly voice, while sniffling and crying. I asked her what her name was. She told me that her name was Leslie, and that she was left by the people who brought her across the Rio Grande River.

I tried to wrap my head around the thought of her making the long and dangerous trip from her country to Eagle Pass, Texas, alone. Leslie said that the group brought her across and told her to walk to the road until she found someone. I assumed that the person who instructed her to do this hoped we (Border Patrol) would encounter her first. Just the thought of it filled me with anger and relief. Anger because she was abandoned, and relief because with the fog and how the road we were on was utilized by tractor trailers, it could have ended badly.

I began to try and get as much information as I could from her to better identify her. The only thing I had to identify Leslie was her name and a phone number for her father that was written on the inside of her sweater with a black sharpie. She stated that her parents lived in the United States, but she didn't know where. I grabbed Leslie by the hand and walked her around the front of my service vehicle and placed her in the passenger seat so I could take her to the station. Leslie was such a mess, that I promised her that I would stay with her through the whole process and for as much of the duration of my shift as possible.

Once we arrived at the station, I began the procedure of processing Leslie as an unaccompanied juvenile. My priority was to try and get her warmed up and fed. Leslie didn't want to eat and was still crying. I was sure being far from home and alone didn't help either. I could tell that that she hadn't eaten, and offered to buy her a happy meal from McDonald's.

Leslie had no idea what McDonald's was, let alone a

happy meal. I understood just how different our worlds were. The next idea I had was to find a Disney movie on my phone and let her watch it to see if that would calm her down. It seemed to be helping a little and it gave me an opportunity start a conversation to take her mind off what was making her cry.

I started talking about Christmas since it was only five days away. I asked Leslie what Santa had gotten her for Christmas last year and she replied that: "Santa doesn't come to my house." If there ever was a statement that delivers a gut punch to your soul, it is hearing a child say that. I don't know if I wanted to feel sad for hearing that, or feel like an idiot for asking and possibly making her feel worse. I reassured her that Santa was real and that he knows that she's here in the United States and also knew where to take her presents.

I moved on from talks of Christmas and on to what she liked and planned to do when she was reunited with her parents. She said that she wanted to go to school, learn English and make new friends. As I finished processing her file, my shift was just about done. I assured her that everything was going to be okay and that the agents who were coming on shift would make sure she was taken care of. I briefed the oncoming shift and they assured her as well that everything would be okay.

I finished my shift, put away my gear and went home with that day's events on my mind. As soon as I got home, I hugged my children tight and greeted my wife. It was days like these that you have to experience for yourself to really know how to react to them. The Academy doesn't train you as to what to do when you find a crying, wet, and cold child who was abandoned. She wouldn't be the first and it sadly won't be the last. I decompressed like I usually do by talking to my wife and telling her about my day. I told her how I found Leslie and about our conversation at the station.

My wife had the same reaction when the topic of Santa and Christmas came up. I told my children the story, and reminded them that that is why they should appreciate and be thankful for what they have, because there are other children who might not have some of the things that they do. They were saddened by Leslie's Santa comment and immediately offered to give up some of their toys.

I told them that we could do one better. We, as a family, went to Wal-Mart that same afternoon to pick out some Disney dolls to send to her parents to give to her on behalf of Santa. About a year later I received a message on Facebook Messenger from an individual who I didn't recognize. It was Leslie's mother. She asked if I was the agent who found her daughter the year before and once confirmed, she gave a big thank you. I told her that it was no problem, that it was my job and that I was glad that Leslie was okay.

A few years passed and that little girl who I found that cold and foggy December morning soon turned into a teenager and then graduated from high school. She messaged me now and then to say thank you and to let me know that she was achieving the goals that she had set out to accomplish.

With any negative attention that our agency receives, and with as low as morale can get, it feels good to know that I made a difference in such a small way. By no means is my story unique in this agency. There are other agents who have literally risked their own lives to save and rescue children like Leslie.

A key misconception is that immigration services like the Border Patrol and ICE only deal with border and immigration issues. While most of the job centers on immigration law enforcement, the Border Patrol routinely apprehends individuals with extensive and serious criminal records as well as fugitives who are on the run from both U.S. and international authorities. Processing is a unique combination of law enforcement, social services, interviewing, asylum determination (not adjudication), and the countless logistical matters involved in housing, feeding, treating, and caring for millions of people each year.

The critical point of misunderstanding in this process is the popular media image that the Border Patrol is *the immigration service*. The reality is that it is simply one component of a large, bureaucratic, and often redundant and contradictory tapestry of agencies all designed to do a nearly impossible thing: to control and protect thousands of miles of land and maritime borders of one of the largest nations on earth, and to deal with millions of people who are attempting to circumvent those borders.

Finally, it is important to understand how the responsibilities of the Border Patrol contrast with other immigration and law enforcement agencies, as well as how the USBP cooperates with those agencies. The Border Patrol is responsible for detection, interdiction, apprehension, and processing of individuals trying to enter the United States between official Ports of Entry. That is where our legal requirements start and end, but as I have explained in this chapter, our basic humanity calls us to do so much more.

The Border Patrol is also responsible for processing those individuals as quickly as possible and either immediately returning them to their home country or turning them over to other government agencies pending judicial or administrative hearings and procedures. The Border Patrol was never designed to be responsible for housing and caring for millions of people or determining the validity of millions of asylum claims.

The U.S. Border Patrol is simply the agency responsible for securing the border, just as your local fire department is only responsible for limited life-threatening events. The fire department does not help you rebuild your home after a fire, nor is it responsible for making sure that the wiring in your home is up to code so that a fire will not start in the first place. Firefighters do not cut down trees that obstruct power lines, and they are not responsible for helping you repair or replace your vehicle after a car accident.

This is why it is critical for the nation to understand what its border agencies are designed to do and what limitations exist before criticizing and vilifying an entire force of dedicated professionals. An informed public is the ultimate defense against political demonization and the decay of our nation's most critical institutions and public services.

4

DRUG AND CHASE

I completed the first portion of my probationary phase of training under the watchful eye of FTO Sanchez. As I described earlier, although we originally didn't see eye to eye on everything, we had finally arrived at the stage where we had mutual professional respect. At the end of the day, I recognized that FTO Sanchez just wanted us to succeed as Border Patrol agents. His methods were not the same ones that I would have used had our roles been reversed, but he was singularly focused on ensuring that we were as ready as we could be when we moved to the on-the-job training (OJT) portion of our probationary phase.

While Border Patrol agents face many dangers when apprehending undocumented immigrants, those dangers increase in intensity when it comes to tracking, finding, and arresting drug smugglers. Border Patrol agents must "sort" undocumented immigrants from drug smugglers. This is one of the most important things we do, because drug smugglers are often armed and, if cornered, might try to take out the Border Patrol agents who try to apprehend them.

In many ways, we were little more than observers and occasional helpers during our field training officer time, and we were kept on a very short leash. That changed dramatically when we rolled into the OJT phase and joined our official unit. There, we worked side by side with Journeymen until we completed our two-year probationary phase and became permanently hired Journeymen ourselves.

I would be lying to you if I didn't tell you that I now felt the pressure to perform. We knew that we had to do our best in the FTO phase or risk washing out of the Border Patrol, but we also knew that the phase wasn't permanent, that we were just "passing through." If we fouled something up, we would learn from it and eventually move on to the OJT phase. But this wasn't the case once we were actually *in* the OJT phase. This was our new home, and if we couldn't hold up our end of the log, that failure would stick to us like glue for years.

My first night on patrol was with a Journeyman named Alejandro Acevedo. He was also a veteran, a Los Angeles Dodgers fan, and was a native of El Paso, Texas. He was a quiet guy, but all in all an awesome partner. We instantly discovered that we had a great deal in common, and this made for easy conversation during our midnight shift.

That night we worked an area called Quemado. It was a heavy dope smuggling area, and we were warned to be especially alert. Thick layers of cane covered the ground, making it difficult to move and navigate. I had an eerie feeling about walking around in the pitch darkness.

Alejandro drove me around and taught me some ins and outs I should know. He had a cool, calm demeanor and seemed unfazed about the potential threat of drug smugglers. Maybe it was because I was the new guy, but I was hyper alert because of that potential threat.

It was about 0400 and we were parked near a red barn, waiting for the camera team to contact us or a sensor to go off in the area. Alejandro pulled out a pad of paper and a pen and started writing. I wondered if he was recording comments on my progress or just taking notes about the job. I asked him what he was working on.

Maybe it wasn't my business to ask, and as soon as I did I hoped he wouldn't get upset. I remember the look he gave me. My old military mentality crept into my head, and I was prepared to get an ass-chewing. "I am writing a note to my wife," he said. That was more interesting than anything I could have imagined. I asked, "Is that something you do often?" He nodded his head in acknowledgment. That was so damn romantic and beautiful. I envied him and the fact that he had that kind of passion for someone.

The next night I was on shift working an area near the Port of Entry. The traffic here moved at a vastly faster pace than at Quemado. Here, people seeking to illegally enter the United States crossed the river and ran to hideout houses or vehicles and almost instantly blended into local civilian traffic. It is literally a cat-and-mouse game. And in most cases, the mice vastly outnumber the cats.

On this night I was riding with a Journeyman named Alfredo Martinez. He went by "Amart" and was as cool as the other side of the pillow. He was well respected by everyone in the unit and was senior to most of us. We knew that because of his star-number. That is the radio call sign given to us based on our order of precedence in the station. Mine was E375. Amart's number was much lower, in the 200s.

We were cutting the drag by the river and saw a group trying to cross. They weren't far enough across the river to make any radio calls yet, so we just shone our light on them from the drag. They were yelling at us because we ruined their plans to cross. In that moment, one of them lost their footing, and I heard shouts of panic.

During my time at the Academy, I learned that many of the people who cross over the Rio Grande can't swim. I found this astonishing. I remember one of the Academy swim instructors showing us a video of two people drowning. One person drowned trying to save his friend, who panicked so badly that he accidentally pulled the man trying to save him under. The video was gruesome. Both men drowned only five feet from land and from a group of screaming friends who couldn't swim.

I was frustrated beyond words watching this video. I couldn't get my brain around the fact that people who couldn't swim would blindly jump into a river. I had been fortunate enough to have been raised with access to a pool and had spent many years at the beach swimming and fighting waves and boogie boarding. I told myself that I would never be able to watch someone drown if I could help it.

The people in the group were screaming in panic. I looked at my partner and asked: "What can we do?" He said that there wasn't much we could do. He radioed to see if any of the cameras watching the river could see if there was any boat crew in the water that could assist. I was frantic. Watching this guy drown was giving me flashbacks of that video I watched at the Academy.

Amart was the senior man, so I asked him if I could jump in to save the guy who was drowning. He said that he didn't recommend it; there were undertows everywhere in the river. I was stunned, but I was adamant. I told him I was a strong swimmer and wanted to go in and try to save the man.

He said: "It's up to you, man." I took off my gun belt and ripped off my pants and top. As I did this, I pulled my hand out of my long sleeve shirt so fast it ripped the cuff off the sleeve. Amart secured my belt, and I jumped in. I knew the initial shock of the cold water would take my breath away, but I was prepared for that. This brought back memories of Ranger School swamp phase in December where I was asked by an instructor to join him in swimming across a river to secure a rope bridge for the platoon.

I started swimming toward the drowning victim. My mind was racing with so many questions. What if he was a bad guy? Was he going to pull me under? If he was a drug smuggler, what was I going to do once I got to him, read him his rights and take him back to the U.S. side? I kept swimming as fast as I could and knew that I was going to find out the answers to all these questions in about twenty meters.

As I got closer, I could see the panic on the man's face. Each

time that I saw his head drop below the water I was worried that
he wouldn't come back up. The current was pushing us down-
river as much as I was gaining on his location. I was about four
feet from him when we both washed up in a shallow part of the
river. He stood up with the water now just above his knees and
I could see that he was grateful to be alive. I stood up, not sure
what to do next. It was an awkward moment with me being in
my boxers and a green undershirt with a shirt cuff around my
wrist.

We were in the middle of the river and it was shallow all
the way to the Mexican side. I looked at him and he looked at
me almost as if we both didn't know what the next move was. I
knew there was nothing I could do, so I started turning back to
the American side. He gave me a sheepish look and then headed
back to Mexico.

I swam back to the U.S. side of the river and was met by a
group of agents who had been watching the entire event. Some
thought I was the biggest idiot for risking my life. Some com-
mended me on the attempt. I was just grateful I didn't watch
that man die without trying to rescue him. I was told to head
back to the station and write a memo on the incident. A memo
is a cover-your-butt paper to document any incident that might
reflect negatively on your career or lead to some kind of administrative action.

This rescue incident became a bit of a folktale among my
fellow agents, with the story told and retold (and changed and
embellished) through the years. As people related the story again
and again, it made me look more like a badass, which was the

furthest thing from the truth. One version had me pulling a drug smuggler out of a sinking vehicle. Another had me rescuing a drowning child. And there were so many more. These stories all sound great, but they are far from what really happened.

Every sector has different methods for tracking groups. In Eagle Pass, there are a few locations where people illegally crossing can get to a ranch, and some where they can walk for hours before coming across a city. Most of the time, when an illegal group enters the Eagle Pass area, they have no idea how far they might have to travel to get to their destination. Many think they will be headed straight to San Antonio, which is almost 150 miles from the border. That would entail a walk of about fifty hours. In reality, the smugglers/traffickers get the group past any significant checkpoints and then load them into a vehicle, which drives them to a holding location at a city with more access to a major highway.

While on a morning shift we were cutting down at the lower drag road and came across a big group. Just from the initial sign, we knew that well over ten people had come across. About an hour had gone by since we started our shift. We tried to confirm, but couldn't figure out the last time this area was cut. This meant that the traffic could be many hours old. By the looks of the sign, these might be "got-aways."

"Got-aways" is a term we use when we track a group as long as we can, and the trail ends at a point where we assume they have been loaded into a vehicle. We determine this by tracking the footprints to a road, at which point the sign ceases without crossing the road. This is a sign that the group has loaded, and we would then report the group as "got-aways."

Every agent hates to report this, but when dealing with such a vast area of operations, we're all painfully reminded of how challenging this career field can be.

My partner and I decided to start pushing this sign. We called for support to see if someone could cut them off or cut a drag road a few miles north so we could get a better line of travel.

A "line of travel" is a relative direction of travel based on multiple identified locations on the GPS. If you track a group long enough, you can get a solid grasp of the identifying landmark they are navigating toward. It could be a water tower, a flashing light on an electrical building, or just about any other obvious point.

As we were tracking the sign, the sun was starting to rise, and it was going to get harder to pick up all the little disruptions of dirt and rocks that the group had made. Another team jumped ahead of us, and they were fortunate enough to identify the same shoe patterns that we were tracking. The forward team was able to start tracking as we returned to our vehicle to leapfrog ahead of them. This was the standard operating procedure for long pushes. We would leapfrog each other to catch up to the group.

As my partner and I started cutting ahead of the team that was on the tracks, we again ran right into tracks in the same pattern, but now they were looking clean and fresh. We knew we were close. By this point, we were fifteen miles from the original entry point at the border. My shift was close to being over, and we had to decide: Is this still good traffic or have they beaten us? If we thought we still had a chance at an apprehension, we would ask the oncoming unit to assist. If we thought that they had beaten us, it would be time to call it a night and report some got-aways.

That night, we kept pushing. It took us a few miles before we started to see some cactus apples that had been tossed half eaten to the ground. These are called eastern prickly pear. They have little, red, apple-looking fruit. We knew we were right on their heels, but I had no idea where we were. This was all foreign territory for me.

We walked another four miles, leading us to another road. Around that time, we had been having trouble picking up sign. This is not uncommon. Perhaps they heard us close on their heels and changed directions. We had called in support from a station called Brackettville, and they were cutting the road and trying to figure out where we had lost the tracks.

I don't know if the people we were chasing got tired of running or were starting to feel the pressure of all the support that had joined us. But they started to pop up all around us, giving themselves up. One after another, they revealed where they were hiding and began to walk toward our vehicles.

All in all, it was a successful night—it demonstrated that training, teamwork, and persistence can lead to success in protecting our borders.

At this point in my Border Patrol career, during this OJT phase, I was making a name for myself. As with most things, the good came with some bad. The *good* was that I had enormous energy and was always motivated to try to find more work than I was actually assigned to do. The *bad* was that I was terrible at Spanish and was always tardy in doing my time card.

Not too long after I "rescued" the guy in the Rio Grande river, there was an incident where we caught a coyote—a person who smuggles immigrants across the U.S.-Mexico border, but also a species of North American wild dog (*Canis latrans*)—with a group of people he was bringing over. After we rounded them up, my Spanish-speaking partner was interviewing the group in the field. He thought he may have identified the coyote, so he had me ask one of the individuals his name.

I walked over to this guy and asked him as calmly as I could: "Como me llamo?" He didn't reply. I was using the motivational: "Ask Tell Make" method that I learned in the military. I got a little louder: *"Como me llamo?"* Again nothing. The man just had a confused look on his face. Now I was getting pissed that this dude was stonewalling me. I have one job to do and it's to ask this guy what his name is. I yelled "COMO ME LLAMO!" as loud as I could. My partner ran over and asked: "Bro, what the fuck are you doing? He doesn't know your name." It was only then that I realized what I was asking him: *"What's my name?"* You can imagine the good-natured abuse I got from my fellow agents. Even today, I still get calls about this.

One night soon after this incident, I was summoned to the supervisor's office. Senior Border Patrol Agent (SBA) Hector Nunez was about five-feet-nothing tall, but he was intimidating as hell. He reminded me of my father, who had a similar build and demeanor. I wanted him to like me, but he seemed to believe, with a background like mine, that I came with an attitude of being better than others. Nothing could be further from the truth.

SBA Nunez didn't even make eye contact as he rattled off the fact that I had now screwed up my timesheet three weeks in a row. He made it sound like I had committed a crime against humanity. He told me that he would not recommend me for Journeyman if I messed up one more timesheet. He told me that being a Border Patrol agent is more than being great in the field and that you have to do the paperwork as well. I agreed with him, and came to realize that I needed that stern talking-to. I had always banked on the fact that I could cover my shortcomings in some areas by being great in others. Now the pressure was on. I have always been good at physical stuff, but paperwork and testing have always been my downfall.

A few nights later, I decided to lay up. Laying up means picking a spot in your assigned area and hiding out to try and surprise traffic crossing the border throughout the night. I picked a location that was known for some fast traffic in the area, and recent intelligence indicated that it might be a good spot.

I was fortunate to have a good bit of assistance that night in identifying targets that might come near my lay-up spot: Carrillo E355. He was one of the best, incredible at using FLIR (heat-signature binoculars) and identifying possible traffic. He was persistent in scanning the area and rarely missed a thing. I was listening to the net when I heard him call in some traffic.

"Copy 920, this is E355. I have five bodies crossing the river. They look like they are carrying long arms." "Long arms" is the term the Border Patrol uses to describe any kind of rifle.

I perked up. I believed that he was talking about a group that could be coming right for my location.

"Copy E355, this is E375, can you confirm the location, and did you say long arms?"

"E375, that is correct."

Then, surprisingly, the radio traffic went quiet. This was not a good sign. I wondered what the hell was going on. I had all my gear and was ready for this situation, but I needed to know whether I had any backup in the area that might be carrying rifles or shotguns.

I radioed: "Copy any agents in the area with long-arm capability."

SBA Nunez came on the net. "E375, this is Supervisor Nunez. Tell me what you need, Vargas."

I replied: "Sir, can I get a few agents headed this way with rifles just in case? I am laid-up in the area and will have eyes on soon."

"Roger," was all he said.

Radio traffic went silent again. It seemed like everyone was waiting for my next move, and all I was trying to find out was whether or not I had backup. I think I'm as courageous as the next guy, but if I'm the only one armed with a rifle and have to take on five dudes with long arms, well, I suspect that you can understand my concern.

"E355 any new information?" I asked.

"Negative 375, but I am almost positive they have armor on from the heat signature."

I was excited to have the opportunity to apprehend what were clearly some bad dudes, but I wasn't sure if I would be able to pull this off if they were armed with rifles. I devised a plan in my head. I was going to push in a little closer and get to a better position. That way, if the worst thing happened, I would have the advantage. My mental math and geography told me that if they kept coming in the same direction, they would walk right into my ambush.

I was channeling my Ranger School training in order to make the best of what was a less-than-ideal situation. In every ambush you need something to initiate the chaos. I didn't have a squad or a platoon, and I didn't have a team with crew-served weapons. All I had was an extra flashlight and a lot of ammo and the burning desire to prove myself in the first potential hostile action I encountered as a Border Patrol agent.

I had trained in engaging multiple targets with speed and precision plenty of times. I honestly believed that if these individuals made it across and for some reason attempted to pose a lethal threat, I could accurately eliminate them within seconds. Shoot-move-communicate, and hope to God my shots were truer than theirs. The reality in any gunfight is accuracy of the shooter and timing of the rounds fired downrange. Who's first to fire and who's more on target?

I have always been willing to die for this. I wouldn't have signed up if I wasn't willing to protect others by sacrificing myself. I knew that there might have been one other guy on the shift who had any kind of combat experience, or who had even been in an engagement, so I wasn't expecting many to jump into this fight. This is literally what I had been waiting for.

I was set up in a good position, with a berm that gave me good cover and concealment. I had my extra flashlight in hand

and felt the adrenaline coursing through my body. My plan was to throw the flashlight onto the road (one is none, two is one), and as that got their attention, it would give me enough time to see if they were armed with rifles or not.

Suddenly, I could hear the cane breaking, and I knew they were close to coming through.

I said, "E355, can you see my location?"

"Copy, I have eyes on."

Just as they broke through the cane, something spooked them. They ran back into the river and made it back to the Mexican side.

In thinking about this, I believe another agent crept in a little too close and scared them. A part of me was relieved, and a part of me missed this kind of thrill that was similar to combat in Iraq and Afghanistan. However, as the saying goes, "There's no harm in living to fight another day." Amen.

When the shift was over and we reported back to the station, I had a chance to meet up with Carrillo and give him huge kudos on how he communicated during the entire situation. He was clear and calm, and that enabled me to get into a good position to engage a possibly hostile group. He shrugged it off with a simple, "You'd do the same thing, man."

Right after that, Supervisor Nunez called me into his office. I thought I was about to be chewed out and possibly fired for screwing up my paperwork again. He told me that I did a good job handling that event and that he noticed how I was able to stay calm on the radio throughout. He told me that I showed some good leadership in a stressful moment.

That meant a lot to me. Maybe *he* was coming to realize that what you do in the field is at least as important as paperwork—maybe even more so. Here is the funny thing. Supervisor Nunez never commented on my paperwork again. Somehow, deep inside me, I knew that my paperwork was likely far from perfect, but he was generous enough to not make it an issue.

A routine *traffic stop* is justified if the officer has a *reasonable suspicion* that the occupant has picked up undocumented aliens or the vehicle is loaded.

One of the most intense actions that can happen in the field is a "failure to yield." An FTY means that for some reason the person in the vehicle decides to run instead of pull over for a routine traffic stop.

During one of our day shifts, working in an area that was a little past Quemado, deep into the Del Rio bordering ranches, my partner and I decided we would go to Moody Ranch for a lunch plate. The Ranch had supported the mission of the Border Patrol and invited local agents to join in on the crew chow. My partner was a senior agent named Raul Munoz. It was his first day back from detail in Ajo, Arizona.

A detail is essentially a deployment to a sector that needs extra agents. Most of the time it is because of an immigration influx that has overwhelmed the sector. The sector requests extra manpower, and agents put in for these details, which can have incentives such as many hours of overtime.

Munoz was showing me the ropes and told me about the Moody Ranch lunches. Day shifts can be busy as we come onto shift because the sun is still rising, but middays can drag because of slow traffic—agents have better visibility and can spot people at a great distance. Said another way, sometimes the sunlight is the best deterrent to illegal border crossing.

This day in particular was moving slowly, so we drove the twenty minutes from our duty location to Moody Ranch. We thought there might be something that bordered the two stations that we were missing simply due to the rural location.

We weren't but ten minutes past Quemado when we noticed a red sedan being loaded with two giant green military duffle bags. We looked at each other in shock: "Fuck, they are loading up! There goes lunch." We flipped a U-turn and went full code: lights and sirens blazing. By then the people in the red sedan realized we had seen them, and the pursuit was on.

"Copy 920, we have an FTY currently on 277 headed toward Quemado, road conditions are clear, weather is sunny and clear. Speed is eighty mph. Requesting to continue the pursuit."

"Copy 287, continue."

As we called in the plates, they started trying to pull away from us. We kept on their tail as we heard the call come back.

"Copy the vehicle has positive hits for possible weapons smuggling." We looked at each other and knew this was going to be a chase.

I put on my vest and checked my rifle. Locked and loaded. We continued the pursuit.

Munoz was calling in the updates as the speeds increased, and things started getting interesting. I imagined if we stressed them out enough, this could end in a firefight. I was excited at the possibility, but also concerned.

We started to get close to Quemado. However, schools were beginning to let out, and we were approaching a school zone. Munoz called in the updates, and 920 requested that we disengage.

The upshot was that while we desperately wanted to apprehend people that were almost certainly drug smugglers, it was too dangerous for us to continue the pursuit through the surrounding community, where we could cause an accident that harmed an innocent bystander, especially a child. We were disappointed, but we understood the decision and supported it.

Sadly, the drug smugglers in the red sedan managed to drive into a local ranch and disappear with their duffle bags with them. We later found the abandoned and empty car.

I tell you this story simply to help you understand that Border Patrol agents are not "rogue cowboys" doing whatever they want to at the border. Rather, they are individuals charged with holding the line while leveraging their extensive training and long apprenticeship.

There are always threats on the border; everyone can be lethal, especially at the river's edge.

One day, my partner and I were cutting the drag road by the river in an area called Local Down, which is known to have particularly fast traffic. By that, I mean it's only about a three-to-five-minute run to the neighborhood to the north. Once an illegal gets to an area where there are houses, they are as good as gone.

As we were cutting the drag, we noticed some fresh signs of two people. We couldn't tell by the look of the prints if they were local fishermen or good traffic. The prints looked wet, as if the people who made them had just emerged from the river. In these areas, it's not uncommon to see U.S. fishermen on the river.

We didn't have much time if it was good traffic, so we started driving north in the assumed path of a possible illegal entry. As we began to zoom to get to the top, we saw two guys wearing old-school orange life vests. They were walking aimlessly. It was confusing to me. I asked them, "What are you guys doing down here?"

They replied, "Fishing."

"What's your citizenship?"

The taller one of the two was starting to get agitated.

"American man, I live right up there . . ." he replied as his voice trailed off.

Then the story got weird.

He was emotional and uneasy, and he said: "We were fishing, and our friend fell into the river and drowned."

The shorter one confirmed his statements with the same amount of concern.

They were now both crying and asking us to follow them to the river and wanting us to help them.

"Please officer, help us, he was right over there."

He pointed toward the base of the river, which was about a ten-foot walk down a slope through the cane. Molina called on the radio for a boat crew to get in the water immediately for a possible rescue.

I was contemplating the rationale behind this whole story. These two were in tears, but for some reason, this all felt strange. My mind was telling me something was off, but the emotions they were displaying seemed absolutely honest.

The taller one stood behind me, telling me to go down to the river, because that's where his friend was last seen. I hesitated and told him to go first. As they both stepped down into the cane and started down the path to the river, they kept insisting that I join them.

Just as I was going to meet them, they jumped into the water and said, "FUCK YOU PUTO!" and swam back to the Mexican side laughing. These two "fishermen" were nothing more than a couple of smugglers who made up this wild story so that they could get away.

What had me on edge was this: What if I did go down to the river? Would they have tried to murder me? Their acting was incredible. It made me uncomfortable to see how smooth their lies were and how in sync they were. This is just another example of the ever-changing threats we face on the border, and it served as a wake-up call for my partner and me not to get complacent.

From that day forward, everyone knew the story and referred to it as Scuba Steve.

While I don't want to overstate the dangers Border Patrol agents face, an incident like this can turn extremely dangerous when the group of people you are attempting to apprehend vastly outnumbers the agents patrolling the sector.

I tended to get partnered up with Carlos DeLeon. He was a young, motivated Border Patrol agent, and a second-generation

Mexican American originally from Colorado. Whenever I knew I was going to work with him, I figured we might have a busy night. We would go cut our drag to start the shift and then listen for any possible traffic in the area that might need some extra attention.

One night we heard a call from within a local ranch with possible traffic. "Copy 1321 had nineteen hits."

Seismic sensors react to vibration and generate what we call "hits." Everything that passes a sensor gives off a measure in numbers. For instance, a sensor will give off a numerical reading. This will provide the agent an indicator of what kind of potential traffic might be in the area. These are relayed over the radio as hits by the camera room. For example, "Copy 1409 had five hits."

If I were the agent working at that location, I would head over to the "bug" (another term for seismic sensors) and evaluate the area. Looking for any sign they might see in the province or in conjunction with the cameras that can view the site, the shift will be able to cancel out local traffic or let us know if the bug is good for illegal entry.

But this night, we had nineteen hits. Carlos looked at me with big eyes. "That's going to be good traffic, bro."

I was too new to correlate the number of hits and whether it was good traffic. So I said, "Dope. Let's go help."

Carlos quickly called Chip, the supervisor on duty, to get permission to leave our assigned area to assist with possible traffic.

Once we got the go-ahead, we suited up and drove over

there. It was the night shift, so there is always a different feel to walking in on a possibly large group in the dark.

If this was my military unit, we would have night vision. But this is the Border Patrol, and their night vision isn't the same quality that we had in Ranger Battalion. Some of the older models were extremely difficult to use since the system was fitted to a helmet. This poses a threat to a law enforcement officer with one hand already being occupied by night vision and the other being ready to deploy if needed. This is a disadvantage when trying to track and be vigilant of one's surroundings.

Once we arrived at the location, we connected with the agents working the area and walked down to the river landing together.

As we got close to the sensor location, we could see sign of a few people in the area. We tried to identify the pattern of the footsteps, but we all ended up going different ways to try and cut off the possible group.

Suddenly, a small group blew past us and jumped back into the Rio Grande river. It happened so fast that I was confused about what had happened. As they started swimming around, they yelled derogatory slurs at us. It was part of the gig. They yelled at us, and we would yell back.

We decided to disengage as they made their way back to the Mexican side.

As we walked back to our vehicles, my partner, Carlos, was still doing some cutting. I could tell he was still unsettled about the whole thing. We both felt that the engagement was off— something was odd about the entire thing. I was thinking it, but based on my lack of experience, and since I had nothing other than a gut feeling, I didn't say anything. Then Carlos spoke up and said, "That was fucking weird."

As we got back to the truck, we heard a call on the radio. "1321 has forty-one hits." Carlos looked at me again with those "oh shit" eyes. We ran back to the bug's location, and there were close to thirty men running back into the river.

Thirty men were somehow hidden in the cane in the middle of the night and had us surrounded. These weren't the normal border crossers tired from a long journey. These men were aggressive and angry that we had interrupted their mission.

I don't get intimidated easily. But thirty aggressive men can quickly overwhelm four agents.

Most of them stopped mid-river and started to talk crap to us. My understanding of Spanish was rudimentary, so I was of no assistance in this back-and-forth debate.

They started talking directly to one agent who was a little overweight, and from what I could pick up and have later confirmed, they were making fun of him. They were telling him to stop acting tough, because if his friends weren't around, they would have gotten away because he was so out of shape.

It was a funny comment for about a second. But the reality of the situation was setting in. If he was alone, this could have had a terrible outcome. He was indeed out of shape, and if they wanted to overwhelm us, he could have been a liability.

The situation eventually calmed, and they returned to the Mexican side. We walked back to our vehicle, all knowing how bad this could have been. It was a quiet, introspective moment.

We all had to self-evaluate, beginning with our choices and night-shift approach.

I had many years of training and experience in hostile environments, but patrolling the border was a new situation for me. I should have been more prepared. I should have expected the unexpected. I knew better, and I went to sleep that night a little disappointed in myself. The overweight agent lost about thirty pounds after that engagement. Maybe it was a coincidence, or perhaps he felt the same disappointment that I did that night.

My career as an agent was now going well, and I was starting to find my way in the unit. I had begun to understand how to determine where illegal border-crossing traffic was active as well as how to use our intelligence unit to help catch dope smugglers. I felt like I was "in the zone."

For Border Patrol agents, dope is the name of the game. Catching dope was like stalking a prized deer and taking a hero shot once you are close enough to do so. The trouble was, at that time, everyone in my unit had had their photo taken with seized dope but me. Anytime I was involved in a dope bust, it was always part of a group effort, and I never really had that feeling that I was instrumental in the outcome. That might not make complete sense to all of you reading this, but for me that photo was a rite of passage.

I was about a year into my time in the field. I had caught groups of people trying to cross the border illegally. I had been involved in several full-on, full-tilt failure-to-yield situations where the people we were chasing decided to try to outrun us. I have been involved in helping others as they led efforts to catch dope smugglers, but I hadn't yet led such an effort. It was beyond time to do so, and I decided to act.

I connected with an agent from our intelligence department and asked him about known dope smuggling routes in our area. He reminded me about an FTY that happened a few months back that involved a female smuggler who was starting to make a name for herself. I remember that she had an interesting nickname—as best as I can recall it was "the Black Widow." When she ran from us, she drove her vehicle full of dope into the river and swam back to the Mexican side with one arm immobile. The intel was that she broke her arm in the accident. She was one tough woman, and from the reports I read, she was very successful at transporting dope loads.

My contact in the intelligence department told me that they had reports that she would be loading up dope in the Quemado area. I just so happened to be working that area with my partner Clifton Hartsfield. He was a very experienced agent and was as motivated as I was to nail some dope smugglers. We contacted our intelligence agent who told us that the Black Widow and her group would likely be coming our way during our morning shift.

We decided to lay up in a spot that gave us the best field of view of two major roads leading into the area that we suspected the smugglers would try to move through. I was suited and booted to the teeth. I had all my gear for hiding in the bushes, waiting for possible traffic. I received a text from my intelligence point of contact telling me that he believed that the smugglers were going to load up the dope in the next few minutes. I was looking at the road when I noticed a white Jeep Grand Cherokee pulling up to a green fence.

I used my binoculars to better see what was going on. As I scanned the area, I saw a girl and a boy, they looked like teenagers, loading several bundles of what I was pretty sure was marijuana into the back of their vehicle. I called my partner on the radio: "We have 46 [our radio code for dope] loading into the back of a Jeep Grand Cherokee on Brian Street."

He replied: "10–4, on my way." I dropped my ghillie blanket (a ghillie blanket is a camouflage blanket that resembles the background and environment such as foliage) and started heading toward the road right after they passed my location. My partner mentioned on the radio that he had pulled onto the road and was pulling up behind the vehicle. Once I got to the road, I saw them put their vehicle in reverse and ram my partner's vehicle. Now it was game on, and we knew we were in for a fight—with kids!

Just then, and unbelievably, they put their Jeep into drive and sped directly for me. When they were about a hundred yards away, I lifted my rifle and started to pie off (methodically moving your weapon in the same fashion that you would cut a pie into slices) to the right to make sure that if I had to engage, I would not be shooting through the vehicle and accidentally hit my partner. I did not want to engage with juveniles. But they were speeding up, and I thought I might have to. I also knew that if I shot the driver, I then had to find a place where I could jump to safety and not get run over.

As I was taking my weapon off safe and getting ready to

engage, the driver and the passenger both jumped out of the Jeep and tumbled from the vehicle while it was still in motion. Thank God! My partner was able to grab the female and I was able to snatch the male. We called for backups, and the cavalry showed up. We had a positive 46 bust with well over eight hundred pounds of marijuana. This was one of the most intense moments of my career as a Border Patrol agent and was an incident where if I didn't react in the nick of time, I might not be writing this today.

I was involved in another failure-to-yield situation that still makes my blood boil. It involved children and drug smuggling.

Drug smuggling has no age requirement. When you live in a border town, it isn't uncommon to hear about friends and family who have smuggled drugs. Even my own extended family has fallen victim to this border reality. For a while, I was teaching mixed martial arts at a local gym. One of the kids I trained, as well as most of the kids I had trained for that matter, have had some connection with drug smuggling. It is a sad reality in most border towns.

Stop and think about this for a moment. Imagine having a ten-year-old son or daughter, and instead of being influenced by you and your partner, their older siblings, your church, their school, and other positive things, they were under the sway of drug smugglers who were teaching them to be criminals. Can you imagine anything worse?

Smuggling can be broken down into several parts. Usually, a drug trafficking organization will pay minors to transport drugs through a checkpoint. Once they get past a checkpoint, there are smuggling roles: loaders and drivers. Drivers make between $500 and $1,500 if the trip is more than six hours.

The average income in Eagle Pass, Texas, is around $37,000 yearly. The average law enforcement officer makes about $47,000 a year. The average Border Patrol agent makes between $65,000 and $75,000 a year.

In a city with a lower income, you can see how it would be easy to decide to smuggle drugs a few times to try to get ahead in life. I don't judge people who do this. Suffice it to say that smuggling is so prevalent in border towns that it is always a challenge for the Border Patrol to make inroads in eradicating smuggling. If there is a demand in America, people will be hired to transport drugs to dealers nationwide.

One day I was processing someone, rolling fingerprints and doing paperwork. As I tended to these administrative chores, I listened to the radio traffic. I heard the calls over the radio of a failure to yield. The agents were chasing a car, but the driver lost control and skidded off the road. As the agents approached, a small-framed individual ran from the passenger side of the sedan and tried to escape.

The radio traffic came through, with the agent referring to the person's stature: "I am on foot pursuit with what looks to be a child. My partner is with the vehicle."

The next call was for a medic or local paramedics. The driver of the vehicle broke his ankle in the crash, and his foot was tangled up with the foot pedals.

Once it was all said and done, the two smugglers were

nothing more than a pair of ten-year-old friends who ditched school to make a little extra cash.

It was the first time I had seen drugs transported by ten-year-olds. I had a ten-year-old child at the time, and I couldn't imagine they would even think of this as an option for making money. My child was setting up lemonade stands and baking cookies to sell.

These boys were products of their environment, and it's not an easy truth to witness. I can't be mad at anyone. They didn't have a mentor in their life as I had who steered them elsewhere. I just hoped that someday they would find their way out of that vicious cycle of border smuggling and trafficking.

People say you can never escape the baggage you bring with you. While that may be true, I also believe in compartmentalization. That is, you focus only on the task at hand and don't think about the past or the future.

When I entered the Border Patrol Academy, I promised my-self that from that day forward I would self-identify as a Border Patrol agent and not as an Army Ranger. I was mostly able to separate the two during my career as an agent, but there were times when bringing back a bit of what I learned as a Ranger was useful.

I spent two deployments in Afghanistan. Afghanistan had a very distinct environment. The look, the smell, the colors. Most of our missions were at night, so I was looking through the lens of night-vision goggles.

My standard combat loadout was my combat boots, my

weapon, my ammo, my gloves, and my night-vision goggles and helmet.

The smells would vary from burnt grass to feces, due to their lack of sewerage systems.

One night on the border, while chasing an individual who was trying to abscond back to Mexico after transporting drugs, I was momentarily confused about where I was.

On that same night, I smelled burning trash nearby.

With the rifle in my hand, the desert surrounding me, and my night vision engaged, I had a moment of: "Holy shit, am I in Afghanistan again?"

This was an indicator that maybe there was something from my combat days that I needed to address before I found myself in a similar situation, but with a worse result.

A few days later, to my surprise, I received an email that my Army Reserve unit was being activated. I knew that I would soon be heading to Fort Sill, Oklahoma, for a length of time. I still had a few days left on my Border Patrol shift as I started to get my paperwork turned in and prepare for military service. My last night shift was with Alejandro Acevedo. We talked and caught up about life.

He voiced his frustration as he explained that his wife's cousin had moved in with them but was overstaying his welcome. He told me that he didn't want to create tension with his wife, so he wasn't going to say anything. It was Acevedo's duty Friday. He would be off the next day, and I would be moving to swing shift.

The next day my partner, Stephanie Hopkins, and I were at

the Popeyes Chicken drive-through grabbing some lunch. Suddenly, we noticed a swarm of police. We decided to follow them to see if we could help. As we started to head down the road, we heard the radio traffic: "Is there anyone who can get to Acevedo's house?"

Stephanie knew exactly where Acevedo lived. We realized that all of the police were headed to his place. We put on our vests and got ready to head in the direction of his house, knowing that one of our own was involved in some way. We both knew it was his day off, and we were confused about what was happening.

The radio traffic came through: "Domestic dispute." I sensed that there was gunfire, but I couldn't get my brain around what was happening. Nothing in my professional experience had prepared me for it. I had nothing to relate it to, and no way in knowing what my plan of action was going to be. It was like a scene out of a cop movie—over twenty cops and several Border Patrol agents in front of the house. As we approached, we saw an ambulance. That was a bad sign, a *really* bad sign.

I could see that Stephanie was getting emotional. Acevedo was one of *our* guys. We wanted to get closer to the house. Sadly, that wasn't going to happen. Our supervisors ordered us to move on and go to our area of operation. They told us that they would contact us if we were needed. I felt helpless and confused. What could have happened?

We found out soon enough. Through text messages and the Border Patrol *chisme* (Spanish for "gossip") network (our unofficial way of communicating about our fellow agents' affairs) we learned that Alejandro Acevedo, our coworker and friend, had been killed in a domestic dispute with his wife's cousin. The information wasn't at all clear as to how the dispute started and what led both parties to engage in a shoot-out.

As more details trickled in, we learned that at some point, the cousin was shooting at Acevedo from the bathroom while he was returning fire from the bedroom as he was putting his kids in a closet to protect them. The cousin was dead at the scene and Acevedo was airlifted to a hospital in San Antonio, but the damage to his body was too extensive, and he passed away during the flight.

There were a ton of rumors regarding this incident, which tend to percolate in a border town. Some said it was the cartel. Others said it was a hit. There were many other far-fetched ideas. But I knew that those rumors were just that—unsubstantiated gossip. Acevedo and I had spoken just hours prior to this tragic shoot-out. I knew there was tension between Acevedo and his wife's cousin. However, what I couldn't understand was how that could have escalated to the point where they eventually killed each other. Something pushed them over the edge, and I don't believe that we will ever really know that answer.

It was a sad day for the Border Patrol, a sad day for our unit, and a sad day for the family. A few days later, we did what any Border Patrol unit would do for their fallen: We had a tailgater. A tailgater in any other world is a BBQ or cookout. That said, for us in the Border Patrol, a tailgater is something we do to hang out with the unit and blow off steam. Sometimes we do this immediately after our shift in our "Border Patrol tux" where we take off our uniform tops and just wear our undershirts and work pants.

We had our tailgater in a location known only to us. We pitched in money for meat and beers and told stories about Acevedo while we drank our sorrows away. It was something I was familiar with from my Army days. I knew what my fellow agents were going through. I had been there before, and I did what I have always done: drank, told jokes, and cried with them.

ALEJANDRO ACEVEDO END OF WATCH
SEPTEMBER 19, 2011, RIP BROTHER

5

DEATH AT THE BORDER

When men and women raise their right hands and pledge themselves for service in the U.S. military, most of them are at least generally aware that they could face combat and risk their lives. This is also true for some other government agencies, such as the CIA, where many Americans have seen pictures of the wall of stars honoring CIA agents who have died in the line of duty.

Most Americans have a view of the U.S. Border Patrol from what they might see on TV or online, but this is a false narrative. It obscures the fact that guarding our borders can be a hazardous undertaking that, sadly, can result in the death of these agents.

It is worth stepping back and remembering that everyone who tries to illegally cross the border is breaking the law. These people have basically said, "I know that what I am doing is breaking the law, but I still choose to do so." When this illegal activity involves coyotes who collect an obscene amount of money from desperate people to sneak them across the border, the level to which they will flout the law goes up several notches. And when drug smuggling becomes involved, the level that criminals will go to in their determination to break the law knows no bounds.

Simply put, drug smugglers have nothing to lose, and if a Border Patrol agent tries to stop them, they must deal with and potentially eliminate that agent. Therefore, it should come as no surprise that in the last two decades, thirty-five Border Patrol agents have died in the line of duty, snatched away from their families and friends far too early.

As I mentioned earlier in the chapter about the Academy, Border Patrol Agent Robert W. Rosas of the Campo Station was murdered while performing his duties on July 23, 2009. Agent Rosas was responding to suspicious activity in an area notorious for migrant and drug smuggling when he was ambushed and, from what was told to me, killed with his own service pistol. This story had played in my head over and over my whole career. This was the first Border Patrol agent death I had experienced during my career, and the grotesque nature of how the killers went about it has given me the chills even today.

I also want to highlight the death of Brian Terry in the line of duty. I have to tell this story in a way that sheds light on the true nature of the event. What follows is the story I have been able to compile over almost seven years of research during my career.

Agent Terry's death occurred during Operation Huckleberry, which was intended to disrupt local rip crews. "Rip crew" is a term used for a group that steals drugs and other contraband. These groups have been popping up more recently over the years in efforts to steal the dope loads that come across the borders or goods from unsuspecting illegal immigrant groups. These small pocket gangs have found the vulnerabilities in the uninhabited deserts along the border.

There is such a vast space in some areas of the border, and these rip crews have been very successful at exploiting them. They are known for being extremely violent because of the nature of their work. They are essentially stealing directly from drug trafficking organizations, and they are prepared to face the consequences with lethal force if necessary. I don't need to tell you that these people are armed to the teeth.

There was an intelligence report that had identified heavy rip crew activity in the Peck Canyon/Mesquite seed trail. BORTAC (Border Patrol Tactical Unit is the SWAT team of the Border Patrol) had developed an operation to interdict these rip crews at a specific point of the canyon.

The original plan was to have an interdiction team and full early warning teams on both sides, north and south, of the X, and for the operation to last a month. After two weeks of long days and longer nights, the teams became exhausted. They thought it was best to cut some manpower to give the teams more adequate work/rest ratios. That decision, I believe, was partly based on complacency and showed unawareness of the traffic that should have been anticipated during the operation.

It is very common for an operation to come up dry. We could have good intelligence and spend many hours planning how to respond to it, but once the operation is underway, it is easy for something to happen that compromises the mission. The factor could be as simple as a scout identifying our activity or a trafficking trail that goes cold. It is not uncommon for trafficking organizations to change their routes.

I can only suspect that the team was thinking about all these scenarios when making their choices. There is no right or wrong in the planning stage. In the military, we say that METT-TC dictates the mission. METT-TC is a mnemonic: Mission, Enemy, Time, Terrain (and weather), Troops (and support available), and Civilian Considerations.

METT-TC includes the relevant factors in operational planning. Another way to phrase this is that your plan of action is always METT-TC dependent. For example, you may be developing a plan to assault an airfield, but if the weather changes, so might your plan. Or suppose you had thirty-six hours to assault an airfield, but due to supply considerations, that timetable has to accelerate to twelve hours. Your plan is METT-TC dependent, and changes to these factors will change your plan.

The unfortunate thing about the decision to reduce manpower in this situation is that it proved to be costly in the most devastating way. On December 15, 2010, a rip crew had approached the designated objective location that BORTAC was focused on. This is exactly the situation this operation was developed for. As the four rip crew criminals advanced closer to BORTAC, BORTAC was able to determine that the rip crew was heavily armed. The BORTAC team identified themselves and engaged with less-than-lethal force. It is important to understand that up until this point, the BORTAC SOP (standard operating procedure) or ROE (rules of engagement) was to initiate with less than lethal force and escalate to lethal force if necessary.

As the BORTAC team engaged, the rip crews returned fire. From what I was told, it didn't take long for BORTAC to transition to lethal force after the initial engagement. But in the chaos of the volley of fire, Brian Terry was hit.

Agent Terry was struck in the pelvis by a round fired by one of the suspects armed with an AK-47. He was flown to a hospital, where he succumbed early the next morning. Brian Terry's loss was the first line of duty death in BORTAC history.

Agent Terry was a U.S. Marine Corps veteran and had served with the U.S. Border Patrol for three and a half years. He had previously served as a police officer in Lincoln Park, Michigan. He left behind his parents, one brother, two sisters, five nieces, and one nephew.

I need to relate these stories in order to make the dangers of guarding America's borders real for you, by telling you about a person, not a statistic. It's important to show how the Border Patrol has had to evolve and come up with better SOPs to enable agents to do their jobs proactively—even aggressively when needed—without putting themselves at extreme risk.

A final reason—and an intensely personal one—to tell Brian Terry's story is to explain how his death influenced my career trajectory, leading me to apply for BORSTAR and eventually serve alongside BORTAC. These were major career decisions that were hugely influenced by the death of a single agent. If losing Brian Terry had a silver lining, his death was a catalyst for BORTAC to become one of the greatest assets to the Border Patrol. His death was the direct reason I made the decision to choose between the two teams.

First, let me walk it back a bit. In earlier chapters I told you about the probationary period we had to endure before becoming fully qualified Border Patrol agents. One goal of this trial by fire was for the Border Patrol to determine if we were really ready to embark on this vocation—this was not assured as there was a substantial washout rate during this period. But another aim was to help the fledgling agent sort out just what they wanted to do in their career.

Some young agents found that there were literally too many choices, and they would simply drift into one career path or another based on completely random reasons. For me, that wasn't the case, and while I was leaning into what I eventually selected, Brian Terry's death pushed me over the line.

I had two years serving a probationary phase before I was eligible to select a specific career field within the Border Patrol. However, in my heart of hearts, I knew that when that time came, I would focus on either BORTAC or BORSTAR.

My father was an EMT firefighter who loved his work. I remember looking through his EMT books with the crazy pictures of cuts and lacerations. I had always known I would go to EMT school at some point because I knew if baseball didn't work out, becoming a firefighter was the next best thing. I went to my first EMT class in junior college. I was able to pass the class, but I never signed up to do the National Registry, something that was needed to keep the certification.

While I served in the Ranger Battalion, I told my sergeant about my extra skill set, and I was given opportunities to take more EMT-focused training. While serving in Afghanistan, I was able to participate in several unique medical situations, such as live tissue training. On my last tour of duty overseas, I volunteered to work at the casualty assistance station (CAS) on days we weren't on a mission.

There, I was able to work on quite a few Americans as well as Afghan nationals, mainly women and children who were injured simply for being in the wrong place at the wrong time and getting caught in a firefight. All too often they were victims of an improvised explosive device (IED) intended to kill or maim American or allied soldiers.

It is hard to describe the feeling of relief and fulfillment when you leverage your training in order to put breath back into a child's dying lungs. When someone asks me today what I did in Afghanistan, I typically don't tell the stories of those medical interventions, simply because most don't want to know the true horrors of war.

These real-life experiences pushed me toward a medical career path in a profound way. After I finished my military service, I completed my EMT course again. This time I took the National Registry of Emergency Medical Technicians (NREMT) certification test. Sadly, I failed that test not once but three times. This wasn't something that I was especially proud of, but given my history of not testing well, it didn't come as a complete shock. Still, I was undaunted in my passion to render lifesaving medical care and make the best contribution I could as a Border Patrol agent.

It was while I was activated as a drill sergeant and serving at Fort Sill, Oklahoma, that we received word of Brian Terry's death.

The news hit me like a two-by-four to the head. When Border Patrol Agent Terry was killed, I had been on the job less than a year. It was a wake-up call for me and for the entire Border Patrol in many ways. For me, a former Army Ranger from the 75th Ranger Regiment, it was hard to imagine going on any lay-up or mission without a medic. Even though many individual Rangers have high levels of medical training, there is always a designated medic on missions. Brian Terry's murder provided a much-needed reminder of the importance of tactical medics, as one was not assigned to his mission. Let me mention that his injuries were severe, and even if there was a medic on target, the outcome would have most likely been the same. However, this is not an excuse to leave a team without the best possible medical coverage on any operation. Terry's murder gave BORSTAR a new focus and the drive they needed to make BORTAC a more complete team for all operations.

There are two special operations groups in the Border Patrol. BORTAC (Border Patrol Tactical Unit) is Border Patrol's version of SWAT, and its selection process is similar to that of Ranger School. Their main mission is running high-risk warrants, but their activities also include sniper operations, breaching, and maintaining high proficiency with pistols. BORTAC is the closest thing to the military in the Border Patrol. It is a close brotherhood with a strong camaraderie, and much like an infantry unit, it is composed mostly of confident, elite, and proud alpha males.

BORSTAR, on the other hand, in my opinion is the best-kept secret in the Border Patrol. It is a law enforcement version of the Air Force's Pararescuemen; BORSTAR agents are highly trained rescue medics who can also manage a rifle. Its selection process is very challenging, and its members receive training in multiple skills. BORSTAR agents have a laid-back style, and when BORSTAR members have been attached to BORTAC, they sometimes have a learning curve regarding how they can most effectively support BORTAC in their role as tactical medics. This is because so many years conducting search and rescue for helpless victims sometimes leaves BORSTAR agents unsure of their roles and responsibilities in a high-intensity mission that is akin to military combat.

There were many conflicting thoughts going through my head when we lost Brian Terry. Up until that point, I had wavered on what my ultimate career path would be. The basic question was this: Should I go tactical or medical? These callings were so different it was almost like being part of two completely different organizations.

If I were to go tactical, it was familiar turf, not completely unlike serving as an Army Ranger. A life of running and gunning was definitely in my comfort zone. Just like in the Army, it would be train, train, train, PT, PT, PT, execute the mission, and then start the cycle over again. I felt like I had done some of the most exciting and dangerous work at the highest level in Ranger Battalion, and I honestly didn't know if the Border Patrol could come close to matching that level of threat and thrill.

When Staff Sergeant Barraza and Sergeant Brehm were killed in Iraq, I remember asking the medics about some of the injuries the two heroes sustained. In both cases, there was nothing that even the most skilled doctors and medics could have done to save them. Same could be said about Brian Terry's death.

The rounds tore into them and damaged the vital organs beyond repair.

With this experience still vivid for me after hearing some of the details of Brian Terry's death, I asked the obvious question: What did the medics do to try to save him? I was astonished and shocked to hear that there wasn't a medic assigned to that mission.

My mind was made up. It was clear to me that medics needed to be part of all potentially dangerous missions that Border Patrol agents undertook. I wanted to be part of the solution that helped rectify this situation. I knew that BORTAC agents and BORSTAR agents often didn't always appreciate each other. I also knew there would need to be a bridge to bring the two together. All the evidence and experience that I had suggested that BORTAC agents were reluctant to fully embrace BORSTAR agents as important players in the tactical world of BORTAC. I also knew that they were absolutely incorrect. I thought that I could provide that bridge by taking my experience of being an Army Ranger infantryman with a wealth of knowledge of combat operations and tactics and transitioning that skill set into becoming a trusted tactical medic in the Border Patrol. That was my new mission, but first I had to apply for BORSTAR and pass their rigorous selection process.

6

BORSTAR SELECTION

While I am mindful that many readers have grown weary of reading the details of the training rigors of various organizations—especially military special operations—I want to take you on a deep dive to explain how individuals are culled from the Border Patrol rank and file and offered the opportunity to try out for a little-known lifesaving service that is unique among all law enforcement agencies. In the next chapter I'll describe BORSTAR operations, but for now I want to explain the process and my struggles of getting through selection and eventually accomplishing the mission of becoming a BORSTAR Agent.

I returned to my Border Patrol unit after completing my one-year military activation as a drill sergeant and was back to work as usual. During my time away, one very cool thing happened. I became a Border Patrol Journeyman while activated in support of Operation Enduring Freedom. To my advantage, my federal time in service didn't stop upon my military activation—the clock kept running. When I returned to my Border Patrol unit,

I had to finish a few tests, but I was officially under consideration for a permanent position. This meant that I was eligible to try out for the Border Patrol special teams. I was now 100 percent convinced that BORSTAR would be my next challenge.

The Border Patrol Search, Trauma, and Rescue (BORSTAR) Unit was created in 1998 in response to the growing number of injuries to Border Patrol agents and migrant deaths along our nation's borders. BORSTAR teams are located at key strategic positions all along the U.S. border.

BORSTAR provides specialized law enforcement, search-and-rescue response from conventional to high-risk Border Patrol operations, Federal Emergency Management Agency (FEMA) mission assignments, national search-and-rescue operations, national special security events, and specialized training support directed by the Department of Homeland Security (DHS) for both domestic and foreign government agencies.

BORSTAR is the only national law enforcement search-and-rescue entity with the capability to conduct tactical, medical, and search-and-rescue training for federal, state, local, and international government agencies. Since the inception of BORSTAR in 1998, the unit has evolved and enhanced its capabilities to better fulfill the missions of the DHS, Customs and Border Protection (CBP), and the U.S. Border Patrol, both domestically and abroad.

I knew that the BORSTAR selection deadline was coming around fast. I felt like I was in good but maybe not great shape. I had been cutting back on running just a little bit. While I had been doing PT daily with the Army, it mainly involved running, push-ups, and sit-ups, due in no small measure to where we were deployed. The BORSTAR PT requirements were similar to those of the Army, but they also included pull-ups and swimming.

During my time as an Army drill sergeant, I got into doing triathlons, which include swimming, biking, and running. I knew that this would help get me ready for the BORSTAR selection process and that competing in triathlons would keep me motivated to continue training, even when the Army basic training PT got monotonous.

As part of this training, I would drive to Lake Amistad and swim as far as I could, working on achieving the best form for the crawl. Then, to mimic the steps of a triathlon as best I could, I would put my shoes on and run two miles, then do a push-up and sit-up workout after that. I would rotate this from time to time, but I would always make sure to train in all these areas in one session to ensure that I was ready for BORSTAR test day.

Being a drill sergeant and having experienced selection processes in the past, I had seen my share of failed PT tests. These weren't armchair warriors who didn't cut it but very fit men. The reasons for this were clear to me: They had always trained the wrong way, and on test day, their bodies simply weren't ready.

The BORSTAR selection process is iterative, with sector and national qualifications. I had about three months to train before trying out at the sector level. The way the process works is that you need to pass the sector physical fitness test to get to the sector selection. The sector selection is designed to ensure candidates are ready before sending them to the national selection process. This saves the hassle of sending personnel who aren't physically and mentally ready for the challenges ahead.

Ranger Battalion has a similar selection process for Ranger School. They send you to pre-Ranger training to prepare you and test your willingness to suffer. Not only did we get smoked daily in pre-Ranger training, but we learned the ins and outs of how Ranger School would work. It made sense to give trainees a selection test first before sending them to Ranger School if they weren't prepared.

I felt ready, but I was no longer a spring chicken—not by a long shot. I went through the Ranger Indoctrination Program (RIP) at age twenty-three and Ranger School at age twenty-five. I was now thirty years old, and I knew that my knees and my entire body would not recover like they used to.

Day one of sector selection was intimidating. About fifty people showed up for the PT test. All these guys were in incredible shape from the looks of it, but I know from experience that even the fittest men aren't always the ones that make it in the end. Selection is a marathon. It was about to begin.

The instructor cadre had us all in a formation inside a warehouse. At the front of the formation was a guy named Nestor Vargas. He was young and in great shape, and he wore a snug shirt to prove it. Everyone knew him, and it seemed like he was the one to look out for. Looking at this guy, I had a moment where I doubted whether I should even be there. I wasn't cut and buff, and I didn't have a six pack. I found myself thinking: *Maybe this special operations lifestyle was behind me now.* Fortunately, I had my Academy buddy Chris Smilo in formation next to me, a friend to share the same insecurities and doubts. Misery loves company, and from my experience, Chris was the best kind of company in these situations.

Memories of all of the selection processes that I'd been involved in during my time in the U.S. military came flooding back. I had the same thoughts, the same doubts, and the same insecurities. The memories were flowing, and out of nowhere I remembered the Cole Range in RIP selection. Cole Range is a field exercise with a curriculum that was specifically designed to "smoke" the trainees through endless punishment via constant physical training. Those were the hardest days of the selection process. It was an all-out mental and physical environment that seemed designed to crush your soul. On what felt like our twentieth mile-long lap being chased by a Doberman pinscher, a Ranger cadre on a quad kept yelling: "It pays to be a Winner RIP."

They kept chanting this while we dug deep to try and finish first, because finishing first meant that you got a break. I remember a soldier named Strickland who was running in front of me. His father was a former Special Forces operator during the Vietnam era. In our world, that was as tough as they make them. Strickland was running right in front of me, cruising along, and all of a sudden he quit. He ran over to a fire where the instructor cadre was making hot dogs and giving out sodas to the guys who volunteered to quit.

It was the cadre's way of psychologically messing with us. They were showing us that it is okay to quit, telling us: "You can be free of the pain." I yelled at Strickland: "What are you doing? Strickland, don't do it!" But he had his mind set—or should I say, his will broken. He had the blood of a hard-core "pipe hitter" (a term used in the U.S. military community to describe special operations personnel, such as the Delta Force, SEALS, the 75th Ranger Regiment, and Special Forces. Pipe hitters are units of some of the most highly respected, well-trained, and qualified operators), running through his veins, but it wasn't enough to keep him in the fight. Everyone has a quit threshold. Some of us are still looking for it. This is what one of my Ranger buddies sent me, and I still recall it today when I need extra inspiration:

Not sure why I thought of this today, and you probably don't remember, but Cole Range was a bitch! I remember it was especially hard on me mentally. I must have broken down like a dozen times over there. Anyways, we were going all out on the road, out in the front leading us, and the Ranger instructor with the Doberman from hell (I don't recall exactly who it was. Maybe Young? Maybe Fader?) calls an amnesty period!

Remember, about five guys fell out. He said that if we had just one more drop we would end this smoke session. He promised us hot chow and a shower. Well I just about stood up. Seriously, I was over this shit at this moment. Right before I stood up, I kinda did a quick scan. I looked to my left, and just a couple rows over, and you had this insane fucking smile on your face.

I knew it was you because of that chin! You mum-bled something under your breath. It was: "Don't fucking quit." or maybe, "Don't fucking do it." I said to myself: "This guy does not give one single fuck!" You continued laughing under your breath. And I thought: "Well, I don't give a fuck either. If this guy can smile while taking this punishment, how much of a pussy would I be if I threw it in here?"

Well turns out, I would go on to adopt this philosophy through every fucking school, every grueling march, every smoke session, basically every time it sucked. I know through your posts that you are battling some shit with your kids. It physically hurts to know a Ranger buddy is going through this. I sincerely hope it works out. Whether you meant it or not, that moment in Cole Range was responsible for a very big part of who I believe myself to be to this very day. I can't thank you enough. I just wanted to share that, and I hope it was cheesy enough. Let me know if there is anything I can help you with. Seriously, just let me know.

This was written to me during the time I was going through a brutal custody battle. I was ready for war; I was prepared to die for anything more significant than myself, whether it was the country, the border, or just about anything that allowed me to sacrifice myself for the greater good of mankind. But I wasn't trained on how to manage a custody battle. I guess that showed in a defeated post on Facebook. My Ranger buddy reminded me of a perspective that I had forgotten.

Back to the BORSTAR selection process. Funny thing, the

order of the PT test was similar to what I had experienced in the Army. Push-ups first, sit-ups second, run third, pull-ups next, and the swim last. Those were the basic parts of the standard physical fitness test. Once we passed those, we undertook the infamous litter carry grind.

We all lined up similar to a military PT test. The instructor cadre got into position to grade the push-ups. Boom! We lost ten candidates who couldn't pass the push-up test. Those of us remaining lined back up for the sit-up test. Boom! We lost eight candidates who couldn't pass the sit-up test.

Now it was off to the run. I knew I would be passing people up, but I wasn't sure how many. Now I was starting to see the diamonds in the rough. I kept seeing the same ten guys leading in the run. I believe I came in third or fourth. I didn't want to kill myself because I was keeping some energy in the reserve tank for the "just in case" crap I have seen in many selection processes. We lost ten more candidates who couldn't pass the run test.

We headed to the pool for the 250-meter timed swim. I looked around to see who was still standing. Chris Smilo had some issues with the sit-ups but was later given a chance to retest. There was that guy Nestor Vargas, much younger than me, who had a slower run. I was starting to gain some confidence again. There was a tall Black kid named Marcellus Smith. He was well known in Eagle Pass, charismatic and cool, and also six-foot-five. As a Black man in a predominantly Hispanic town, he stood out. There was a muscular white boy named Michael Crowley. He was in the top five in every event. He looked tough and confident. I expected that he would be going to pre-selection with us. There were a few others who stood out too, especially a few Hispanic kids who looked super young.

As the swim test started, several guys requested to drop due to injuries sustained in the run. I took my swim test, but again saved some fuel in the tank. Once we passed that test, the instructor cadre told us to go change into duty uniforms and head outside to wait for whatever was coming next. I got dressed as fast as I could and started heading outside.

As I did, I took a look back at the pool to see who was testing. I saw someone really struggling. The cadre was yelling at him, telling him to keep pushing. As I left the pool area, I noticed it was Vargas, and it turns out he didn't finish the swim in time. It is always sad to watch someone give all their effort and fall short.

The remaining seven guys were taken to an open road outside of Del Rio. The litter carry was next. I was ready for it. At one point in my life, I was training to be a pararescueman. During their selection process they carry water jugs as a proxy for a litter carry. A litter carry can be extremely taxing on the forearms, shoulders, grip, and legs. Essentially it was all about carrying a simulated patient for a long period of time. No matter what the patient's condition is, you can't fail that person. You have to work as a team to give each other breaks to rest and rotate jobs.

We did this drill for about five miles before the instructor cadre shut it down. We now had the seven guys that would be going to pre-selection and preparing for national selection. There were a few candidates who had come close to passing scores, so BORSTAR management made the decision to allow for a retest for those individuals, as well as a makeup test for one military member who was on military orders during the original test date. Eventually, we went into the pre-Academy with eleven trainees.

Special Operations is a small group–oriented team, and the last thing you want to do is bring in a toxic individual who would be a cancer for the team. Before we got through to the pre-selection, the BORSTAR team did their due diligence to "cut sign" on all of us. They wanted to know who had a good reputation in the field, and more importantly, who had a bad reputation in the sector.

Throughout the next two weeks, several people either volunteered to be removed from training or failed to meet the BORSTAR pre-selection standards. That year, Del Rio Sector sent seven candidates to the national selection.

The seven of us headed to the selection site in San Diego, California. We were going to a small island called Coronado. Most might be familiar with this place, as it is the location of the Naval Special Warfare Command where Navy SEALs go through their training. We moved into the same barracks as the SEAL candidates going through the BUDS (Basic Underwater Demolition/SEAL) training.

Looking back on that aspect of our training years later is a bit of a blur. What I *do* remember was getting on a bus and heading to a place called Glorietta Bay. Once there, we checked our gear and waited for everyone to get there. It was the calm before the storm. I remember getting our number identifier. That was the participant number based on alphabetic sequence. My number was eighty-three.

Once we received our numbers, they took us back to the

SEAL barracks, and all hell broke loose. The cadre was dumping our gear, looking for contraband. They found so much stuff that I couldn't help but believe that they planted it just to make us pay. This cadre was worse than a new Army drill sergeant who just graduated from the Academy. They smoked us for hours and hours as if they didn't give a damn that we had a PT test the next day.

Once the smoke job was done, they gave us so many impossible tasks that I knew we were in for a long night. From cleaning the barracks, to lining up our gear bags, to delegating fire guards, to assigning bunks. It was meant to kill any time we thought we might get for sleep. This is a common thing to do in selections. If you can't introduce real-time stressors, you have to create them by taking away common comforts like phones, families, sleep, and food, basically, all those items we have grown accustomed to having easy access to.

But of all the stressors, lack of sleep was the crippler that could make the strongest men question everything. It was maybe 0300 when we decided to bed down and deal with the consequences in the morning. The room was trashed, the tasks unfinished, and I was making every effort to be the gray man again for as long as I could. Getting through this next day meant everything. I needed to get through the PT test, swim, and litter carry the next day. After that, it was all about having the intestinal fortitude to keep pushing. I closed my eyes and tried to be ready for what was to come. It didn't take long.

At four in the morning we heard: "WAKE UP!" The instructor cadre came crashing in with a vengeance. I woke up to what felt like déjà vu. I jumped off my bunk to get dressed, but before that I was so disoriented that I grabbed the guy next to me and yelled at him: "What course is this?!" He yelled back: "BORSTAR selection!" Now it was all making sense. I had been to so many courses in my career, especially ones with rude awakenings in military barracks, that I was confused as to what course I had just time traveled to. I told you that lack of sleep was a stressor, and I was living it.

This episode was textbook Army drill sergeant. One of the instructor cadre was holding an aluminum trash can, banging it and yelling, stressing everyone out. We scattered like cockroaches trying to find a place to hide. I grabbed my shit and headed out to formation. On my way out, Ricardo Baccera stopped me, looked me in the eyes, and said: "Bro, I didn't even sleep." The look in his eyes showed absolute disbelief. I didn't want to scare him by saying that this was likely the most sleep we would get for the next three days.

The PT test was just like the pre-selection. It had the same fallout rate, but this was on a national level: We were seeing the cream of the crop of each sector taking the PT test and dropping like flies.

That day ended with more than a third of the class headed back to their sectors. Every night ended with a similar punishment. We would get in formation and get dusted off for hours and then released to our rooms for a night of impossible taskings. This now included two "Rescue Randys," meaning that Rescue Randy would be our litter carry patient throughout the rest of the selection process. The Rescue Randy manikins were easily over one hundred pounds per litter, and on top of that, we also had to lug our water supply in ten 5-gallon water cans.

This was an effort to wear us down throughout the day and to get us prepared for the worst possible event in a BORSTAR agent's career: a litter carry from deep in the border and no relief in sight. Being that our job can occur in austere environments, this is the mecca for a "shit has hit the fan" scenario. Prepare for the worst, and hope for the best.

The funny part of all this (funny in retrospect, not so much while happening) was that while *we* were getting dusted off by our cadre, so was the next BUDS training class. It was one big pissing contest between cadres of opposing forces. I realized how this was a huge disadvantage for our class. The cadre wouldn't just copy what the BUDS instructors were doing, they would try to top them, all to make our lives as miserable as possible.

There were a few things that I was able to implement in the barracks to make our life a little more bearable and streamlined. I helped create some SOP boards to organize our gear, figure out morning cleaning details so we wouldn't get dinged on the cleanliness of the barracks, and organize the fire guard roster. These were all small items and things that I learned in my years in the military and through innumerable training courses.

I remember having a meeting with everyone and explaining that no matter how perfect we are, the cadre will always find a reason to smoke us. I told them that we didn't need to get emotionally invested in the small details of why they were doing this but instead focus on why we wanted to become BORSTAR agents so badly. If we concentrated on the prize, we wouldn't allow the cadre to destroy our morale.

As the days passed, the smoke sessions got worse, our sleep was disturbed even more routinely, and our class grew smaller. We had now lost three of the Del Rio Sector guys we started with. Baccera had a knee injury that eliminated him from the course. I don't know how bad it was, but I knew the entire experience was overwhelming for him. Arnold Noyola was failed during the pool portion of the training. There were moments that the cadre would splash the perfect amount of water down your throat during some difficult portion of the water training. I wasn't there, but I think this is when they pulled him out of the pool and sent him back to his unit.

Jamie Villareal had always had issues with the pool, so much so that in the pre-Academy I would hold his shorts during treading water portions of the training to keep him from sinking. He would repay me with extra sandwiches his wife made. Those sandwiches were the best. Villareal was as solid as they came, and I would have done anything to help him, but I wasn't with him the day he was pulled from training.

Now there were just four of us left from Del Rio Sector, and we wanted to keep it that way in order to salvage our pride, not just individually but also for our sector. The instructors did everything they could to get us to quit, and on day seven they almost had me.

I have never been in a situation in my military career that would have made me quit. The hardest thing I had done before joining the military was hell week in football. Hell week was a weeklong physical fitness and football-simulated exercises that would push most high school kids to the brink of quitting. During Army basic training and beyond, I had never let the idea of quitting cross my mind. Even when pushed to my limits, I had always continued to push forward and find a way to power through. That is, until day seven of BORSTAR selection.

My knee was starting to swell. It was painful to bend and agonizing to run on, but it was still working. As I started to fall out of the morning PT session run on the beach, the cadre started to punish everyone for my lack of ability to keep up. They would yell: "Say thank you to 83," and, "How does it feel 83, to know you are the weak link?" Those words on any other day of training would fall upon deaf ears, but on that day, at that moment, it was the excuse that I needed to just stop the pain.

I was feeling defeated, and for the first time in my life, I contemplated quitting. It was an emotionally painful thought. I kept wondering what my kids would think of me. How would my father react to me? Would he say that I wasn't tough enough? How would it feel to face everyone back at my unit who, up until now, believed in me?

A cadre instructor named McCardell was in my ear the whole time. He was playing good cop, bad cop, and was going all psycho on me. As bad cop, he yelled things like: "Quit 83!" "You aren't good enough!" "Go Home 83, we don't want you!" Then he switched to his nice guy persona, saying things like: "It's okay 83, you don't want to permanently hurt yourself; it will ruin your future," and, "The van's there man, just quit, it's cool."

I admit that I was about to quit. My eyes were watering.

I was breaking down, and the voice in my head said: *Fuck, I might actually quit.* I can't tell you what it was, God or ego, but just as fast as this desire to quit penetrated my brain, the anger followed. Without breaking stride, I turned to McCardell and said: "With all due respect, sir, you can keep yelling all you want, but I won't quit." I was able to close the gap and get back with the group, and thank God the run ended.

At day nine or ten we got a two-day break. Each of us sorely needed it. We had to lick our wounds and reorganize ourselves. When we returned, the instructor cadre took us on a beach run. It was an easy jog. As we approached the entrance of a pier, they started mentioning that we needed to pair up strong swimmers with weak swimmers.

Marcellus Smith was a great runner and a weak swimmer; I was the opposite. We partnered up and moved to the rear of the formation. I wanted to be able to see what they were getting us into so that we could prepare as best we could. We started slow jogging to the farthest part of the pier. I was confused as to what was next. Smitty looked at me in disbelief. Were they going to make us jump? I told him: "There's no way bro." There are signs about every ten feet saying that it is a federal offense to jump off the pier. I told him they were just messing with our heads. This is a common practice in any special operations selection. Mind games can cause some individuals who are teetering on quitting to make an ill-informed decision that they will regret the rest of their lives.

Just then, I saw the instructors begin to jump in, and then, in buddy team order, the next group and the next group followed.

The drill sergeant in me was assessing the safety precautions in place to mitigate any potential hazards that would kill me. There is no way that this was approved, I told myself. But Smitty and I walked up to the end of the pier and jumped!

It was a long fall and felt like forever. Once we hit the water, the shock from the cold took my breath away. I swam to the top to catch my breath and grasp what was going on. We had jumped into freezing water with high tides, and now we had to swim a mile to shore. I'm a strong swimmer, but everything about this had me concerned. Smitty wasn't a strong swimmer and this situation made even a strong swimmer like me less confident.

I was trying to explain to Smitty during the swim how to manage the waves. Over many years of boogie boarding, I had learned a few things about getting under waves when you find yourself in a bad spot. At first, Smitty was a few feet from me. We started swimming toward the shore, and we could see the sea swell and start to form a wave. I yelled over to Smitty to get ready and get under it. As it started to peak, I knew we were fucked. I ducked as low as I could, but the force of the wave pulled me into its spin cycle, or at least that's what it felt like: being put into a washer and flipped head over tea kettle time and again until you don't know which way is up or down. I finally came out of that spin, and I immediately looked for Smitty.

He was now about twenty feet from me and was frantically looking for me as well. I heard the tone in his voice, and that's when I really started worrying. I could tell that he was just as nervous as I was. He yelled "Vargas!" I yelled back as loudly as I could: "Here comes another one!" But he didn't react.

I believe it's called a duck dive. I was yelling: "You have to get under the wave! Here it comes!"

The waves felt like they were twelve feet high and coming in groups of three. This was number two, and it flipped me just as hard as the first one. I tried to catch my breath and keep Smitty in my sight in case the waves put him in the spin cycle I had just experienced.

To be completely honest with you, I could feel things deteriorating rapidly and was now flat scared. I was extremely nervous about this situation because at this point, I wondered if I would be able to save myself, let alone my friend. The third wave hit us, and it was at least as powerful as the first two. By this time, I was exhausted and needed a small break to get my head right. I knew we had a moment before the next wave. I told Smitty we needed to swim our asses off so we could get closer to shore and to a point where it was shallow enough that we could at least stand up.

We swam toward shore as fast as we could. We got hit by a few more waves, but I didn't feel there was a threat anymore since we could at least touch the bottom. We made it to the sand and licked our wounds, then hustled up and got back into formation. I don't believe we lost anyone on that day.

The instructor cadre made BORSTAR selection a trial by fire that few of us would want to endure again. That said, I would be remiss if I didn't give a shout-out to one of the cadre by explaining how dedicated these professionals are to making us the best BORSTAR agents we can possibly be.

There were some significantly in-shape cadre members I

eventually taught alongside in future academies. But I can't talk about my time in the BORSTAR selection without mentioning a standout cadre member. He was the lead PT instructor for the course, and his method was a show of force if I have ever seen one.

I don't want to take any praise away from the other cadre members who taught alongside him, but I feel, for some reason, that Alan Rogers had a presence about him that will forever be locked in my memory.

Alan Rogers was a fit Ken doll mixed with R. Lee Ermey's drill-sergeant character from *Full Metal Jacket*. He wasn't belligerent or even vulgar, but he could easily ramp up the intensity. He did this thing where he would slowly unbutton his sleeves and then slowly unzip his jacket and strip down to his green shirt. That process alone had guys quitting because they knew that a Rogers smoke session was about to go down.

There was a wheel on a piece of wood that we would spin at the end of the day to see what our physical training would be before we were dismissed for the day. Written on the wood was "The Wheel of Misfortune." Talk about a pit in your stomach as you watch every exercise you have come to identify as punishment tick-ticking to the next even more painful exercise as the wheel spun.

We did this every single day of the selection process. Sometimes Rogers would stop the wheel on the exercise of his choice just to make things hurt a little more than they already did. He showed no remorse and no empathy. It was pure unadulterated crushing souls and taking numbers.

On one of the days we had managed to stay off the beach, and we were hoping to land something that wouldn't get us wet for the night. It was becoming hard to keep our boots dry and free of sand. The roaming granules had already caused significant discomfort of a kind I had never experienced before in a selection process. Where there is sand, there are abrasions and chafing.

He called up the students to spin "The Wheel of Misfortune." Tick, tick, tick, ticking to a destination we can only pray contains an "easy" exercise. As we watched and tried our best to create a telekinesis effect on the wheel, it came to a stop on the one we had been praying for.

We cheered our asses off at the fact it landed on EASY DAY.

As we were celebrating a small victory in a place filled with low morale where we couldn't seem to recover from soreness fast enough, we noticed Rogers unbuttoning his sleeves.

In a typical training environment, this would be cruel and unusual punishment. But in Special Operations selections, this is the norm. This is how you break people's will. You lead them on to believe the run is over, the pain is done, the punishment is completed, and as soon as the students feel like they have relief and light at the end of the tunnel, you continue to punish them into submission. This is a typical mental "fuck you" in all selection processes.

In the Ranger Indoctrination Program, we ran a hard five miles, fast and furious. We knew the route, so I knew when we were getting close to the end. As we started to slow down near the finish line, we turned around and went for another mile. Guys were dropping like flies. It was the most effective way to break someone in a selection process. I told myself never to get excited or expect any kind of relief in any section from that day forward.

And here we were, many years later, and I got just as excited as any other candidate when the wheel landed on EASY DAY. I forgot my own rule.

Rogers started warming up by jumping onto the tail of his Chevy work vehicle as if it were a box jump at the gym. The noise was intimidating, but was secondary to the visual of the truck almost bottoming out as he landed. He mumbled to himself: "Easy day; easy day."

"You want an easy day? I got your easy day. Follow me," he said.

I knew it was about to get medieval. Rogers was the type of character they made movies about. He was relentless and almost neurotic. He wasn't just yelling at us to do an exercise; he did every repetition with us.

We ran to the cold Coronado beach. The dry clothes we were excited about wouldn't be dry for long.

Rogers ran into the water, and we followed. He ran out of the water, and we followed. He dropped and rolled into the sand, and we followed. "Make yourself into sugar cookies," he said, using a term that was made famous by the Navy SEALs.

We rolled around, low crawling and moving left and right. He got up and ran back to the original formation as if the session was done, and then turned around and repeated this three more times.

By the time he was actually finished, the other cadre had shown back up—dressed for the dinner they had reservations for, and they realized Rogers wasn't going to be ready in time.

He released us back to the barracks to dry off another pair of boots, clean the sand out of the nooks and crannies, and try to get some sleep.

Rogers was an absolute legend in my eyes.

This was just one of many smoke sessions and gut checks. All in all, by the time we got to graduation, we had several recruits drop due to hypothermia, injury, and just realizing that this line or work wasn't meant for them. But those of us who were able to power through selection week graduated as better men, women, and agents.

I had enormous respect for the people and processes I encountered during my time in Ranger Battalion, as well as during my service as an Army drill sergeant. After going through the hell of BORSTAR selection I now had equal respect for the Special Operations component of Homeland Security.

Agent Arnold Noyola eventually made it through the selection process to become a BORSTAR agent and is currently the Unit Commander for the Del Rio BORSTAR team. Agent Jamie Villareal is one of the members of that same team. This is a testament to kinds of professionals we have on these teams. They regrouped, retrained, and found a way to pass the course and become a part of the team.

When people read my "résumé"—athlete, Army Ranger, BORSTAR, etc.—they immediately assume that I am a supremely confident guy. However, I am not. I am just me. As I've mentioned, I had some speed bumps during BORSTAR selection. I was *truly* worried that I would wash out. That is why it was so gratifying to read this note that one of our cadre members sent me years after the fact:

So in week one we discussed if PT was gonna take you out. Admittedly I was skeptical and thought you'd tap out. About week two we started seeing your leadership and how the other candidates looked to you consistently. I specifically remember one night the cadre were headed out and we stopped by to pick up Alan from your barracks. It was the night we made a candidate cry with a simple math problem. I noticed MRE boxes with the Academy backpacks drawn on them with a proper packing diagram from the front and both sides to make your packs uniform. Not sure how we found out you had done that, but it showed your experience, ingenuity, and leadership. Alan continued to bear crawl y'all for the rest of the evening while we went out on the town. Another incident that showed leadership was when we tossed y'all's barracks, you took charge and had the room cleaned up in the time hack, which is seemingly impossible as you know.

Grit—you had a lot of grit, not sure how you made it through the PT sessions half the time.

Eventually we went from: Is this guy ever going to tap out, to this class is screwed without him. You were affectionately referred to as the class's Papa Bear.

Not sure if you remember the: "In the Army we go both ways" incident in formation, or the Vargas and Dorsey comedy show before we cut y'all, but those all stick out in my mind.

—Patrick Limbaugh

7

BORSTAR

As I mentioned in an earlier chapter, BORSTAR was created about a quarter century ago to deal with urgent medical issues of migrants in distress as well as injuries to Border Patrol agents. BORSTAR is located at the U.S. Border Patrol's Special Operations Group (SOG) Headquarters in El Paso, Texas.

From the time I became a Border Patrol agent, I had my eye on BORSTAR and aspired to join. It seemed like the most righteous work I could do—protect our border while simultaneously rendering aid to the most desperate and vulnerable people who had, literally, no one else that cared whether they lived or died.

Although BORSTAR selection was its own little hell, there was a silver lining to that time: It gave me a deep respect and appreciation for how well the instructor cadre prepared me and my fellow fledgling BORSTAR agents for what we would encounter in the field.

If you have never heard of BORSTAR, here is a bit of blocking and tackling that explains what the unit does.

The key words here are search and rescue—getting to people before the elements claim them. The tragic death of fifty-three migrants who were inside a semitruck near San Antonio in June 2022 tells you all you need to know about the extreme temperatures at our southern border, as well as the cavalier attitude of the coyotes who bring them here. More on the coyotes in a bit.

As comprehensive as the BORSTAR selection process was, once we completed that and arrived at our units, there was even more training we needed to accomplish, and it was intense. We received advanced specialized training in emergency medicine, tactical medicine, technical rope rescue, helicopter rope suspension, rescue watercraft/boat operations, personnel recovery, tactical combat casualty care, and advanced dive, swift-water rescue. With all that training, I wasn't the only BORSTAR agent who had a bit of a swagger.

Once we graduated from the BORSTAR Academy, we all were sent back to our sectors. The Del Rio team went back to work on some of the issues in our area of operation. During that summer, 2012, we lost close to sixty migrants trying to cross the border. The heat can be unforgiving.

The reason for these deaths is easy to understand. Most border crossings happen at night, either with coyotes dumping people once they make it across the border or people finding their own way across without knowing anything about the geography or terrain. By the time the sun comes up, it's almost too late for them if they haven't been able to find significant shelter.

The reason these people are so vulnerable—and where

BORSTAR agents are crucial in helping save lives—is that many of these people purposely *don't* seek shelter because they think if they lay up somewhere, they will be sitting ducks for the Border Patrol. These are the sad realities of it all. These desperate people are willing to risk their lives for the chance to come to America, and their way of doing so actually causes many to lose their lives needlessly.

That said, it wasn't my job as a BORSTAR agent to judge anyone on their efforts. It *was* my job to conduct search and rescue and provide aid and, where needed, lifesaving intervention before any human life was lost in the unforgiving terrain of the Texas border. I think you can see why my fellow BORSTAR agents and I were always keyed up: We knew that time was never on our side.

I want to take this moment to explain why a group of migrants would be scattered and left to die. On the Mexican side of the border there are organizations whose sole purpose is to extort the desperate and uneducated by offering them a way to gain illegal entry into the United States. These people charge exorbitant fees that must be paid in advance.

Once they have this money in hand they manipulate, threaten, and often abuse their cargo while in transit. It is not uncommon for families to force their young daughters to take birth control pills so they don't get pregnant if they are raped by the smugglers, something that happens all too often.

Therefore, it does not require a logical leap to imagine these evil people typically abandoning migrants once they get them across the border. If you don't live along the southern border in California, Arizona, New Mexico, or Texas, it is difficult to explain how easy it is for these people to get completely lost and wind up wandering for days and days in a place with no shelter, where temperatures typically exceed one hundred degrees on most summer days.

That is why BORSTAR agents are so motivated to find those people who have been left behind by these organizations or coyotes. Coyotes have absolutely no reason to make sure the *pollitos* (chicks in English and a term used to describe the individuals being smuggled) make it to their final destination. They are paid to make the effort to get them just across the border, and they do that not because they are humanitarians but because it is good for business. If they are successful in getting people across, then their "customers" will communicate with others in Mexico and recommend that coyote to others wanting to cross.

But after collecting their initial (huge) fee to get a person across the border, coyotes continue their extortion, saying things like: "We will help you get across, and we can also provide you with this nifty bag with day-to-day items that will make your journey smoother. It will cost you just an additional $19.99." Their methods remind me of those used by merchants in Afghan bazaars. These organizations view desperate individuals simply as a source of income and not as humans. This is why, at the first sign of trouble or upon seeing a Border Patrol agent, the coyote will turn and run south, leaving his paying clients to fend for themselves.

The BORSTAR motto is: "So Others May Live." This is embodied in BORSTAR's full name: Border Patrol Search, Trauma, and Rescue. Its singular mission is to save lives. It doesn't matter what color your skin is or where you are from. If your life is in danger and we come across you, we will do everything in our power to save you.

My very first day on the job as a BORSTAR agent was dedicated to finding a group of scattered migrants at night. Smilo and I were riding together in our new special operations uniforms. It felt just as good as putting on the tan beret in Ranger Battalion. We were pumped because, just like combat medics in the U.S. military, we could save lives.

We were deep into a ranch and cutting a drag road. We noticed some footprints that looked clean and very recent. We knew from the time frame that this could be part of the group that had scattered earlier that night. We parked the truck and proceeded on foot in the direction of their travel.

Smilo called in the traffic. He told the operations center that we had found some sign, but we weren't sure if it was still "good traffic." Within seconds of that radio call, we stopped in our tracks and noticed a red shirt tucked under a bush. As soon as we noticed that one, we started to pick up a lot more colors in between several other bushes all around us. It reminded me of an Easter egg hunt.

What we discovered was that this group of people was asleep during the middle of the day just to try to get out of the heat. That day, the temperature was in the high nineties. It is completely possible that some of them could have died of heat exhaustion if we hadn't spotted them. We started pulling them out of the bushes and lining them up.

Smilo and I were stunned as we continued to pull these people out of the bushes. The count kept getting higher. Ten turned into twenty, and twenty turned into forty before we knew it. We radioed for backup, and before long we had a helicopter overhead and the rest of the team came to help us.

What surprised us was how far we were from the actual border. It was strange—even bizarre—to find such a large group of migrants this far past the border. It was easily a four-to-five-day walk from the border to this point. They all needed water, and to get out of the stifling heat. I do not doubt that we saved several lives that day.

As months went by, we rescued many additional people. It tore at my heart how desperate these migrants were to find a better life in America, that they crossed the border with little idea of what they would do or even where they would try to go. It was like trying to go treasure hunting without a map. They had too much trust in a system that cared very little about their well-being.

One night I was at a restaurant and found my team leader, John Parham, there. We had become close over the previous year because of his love for boxing. My father was a well-known professional boxing cornerman, and I spent a fair share of my childhood around boxing as well as sparring with my older brother or other neighborhood kids. In the military, one of my skill sets was serving as a combatives instructor (meaning use of force and hand-to-hand combat).

Parham and I had sparred several times, and he had helped

coach the Border Patrol boxing team. We were cut from the same cloth. This was his night off, but I was on twenty-four-hour recall, so I couldn't drink. John was already a few beers in when I got the call. There was a search-and-rescue mission in close proximity to my location about forty-five minutes away. I canceled my order and gave John a hug and headed to my house with my gear.

Within fifteen minutes I was on my way to the location relayed to me by my commander. I was given the basic information for the mission. A lost person had called 911 and had asked to be rescued. This individual said that they were feeling sick and had not had any water or food for quite a while.

A few weeks prior, my team had been on a similar callout, but by the time they got to the original location, the lost individual wasn't there. From what they were told, the person who had called was suffering from dehydration and also likely hyperthermia, so they probably wouldn't be able to follow any instructions in such a state of distress.

During that mission, the person, a female, had continued to wander off looking for relief. Sadly, by the time the agents were able to locate her, she had died due to exposure. This isn't uncommon, so that's not why the story remains in my head. The woman had pulled her clothes off and spelled "HELP" with sticks. I saw a photo of the sticks that an agent had taken at the scene, and it stays with me still.

This was at the front of my mind as I approached the location. I noticed footprints leaving the area and realized immediately that this might be a long night. I parked my rig and put on my pack. I had water—lots of it—flashlights, and my med bag on my back. It was time to start tracking with purpose. I couldn't help but think of that woman and the sticks.

It took me about two hours of tracking, and by that time about four other BORSTAR agents were in the area, cutting sign nearby. I finally saw him. I could tell that he was wobbling because his footprints had become sloppy. I could also tell he was beginning to struggle to walk. I was able to get to him in time to administer fluids via an IV and give him some food to tide him over. After a long night searching, it is always a relief for the team to have small victories.

BORSTAR agents were equally in demand—maybe more so—when we were tasked with water operations. One of the reasons that the BORSTAR Academy stressed water operations so much is that there was a high probability that BORSTAR agents would, at some time during their service, be called upon to rescue people stranded in the Rio Grande river.

The Rio Grande is a no-kidding, dangerous, swiftly flowing river. The speed of the river often reaches six miles per hour. Not only that, but rip currents are common, which extend from near the shoreline, through the surf zone, and beyond the line of breaking waves, and can completely overwhelm even an accomplished swimmer.

I've already mentioned that the desperate people trying to cross the Rio Grande weren't even competent swimmers, let alone accomplished ones. Knowing this, as part of my mental preparation when I drove to work every morning, I imagined what it would be like if I had to plunge into the river and rescue a helpless person.

I approached a group that came across the river moments prior to me responding to agents requesting help. When the illegal immigrants saw me, I yelled to identify myself. It spooked them, and they scattered. I was able to apprehend one of the individuals. The others jumped into the river and headed back south. As I was securing the individual I had apprehended into my transport vehicle, the group that fled south was yelling at me in Spanish. From their tone, I knew they had a serious issue.

One of their friends was being pulled under by what I can assume was a rip current. I hurried back to my truck to grab my rope bag and ran to the river's edge. I submerged my rope bag and threw it in the last location I saw him, but he never returned. His body was discovered a few days later. These are the hard memories that will stick with a rescue agent forever.

Well, things don't always work out the way you plan them. Soon after this river rescue there was another water incident with a completely different outcome. This time, I was home with the kids when I got the call. I rounded up the kids and packed my gear and headed south for a potential swift-water rescue mission.

Any time there's a callout, no matter the scenario, I am always thinking the same old things. Will this be the mission that kills me? Will I see my kids again? Will I be able to save someone in desperate need? It's not easy to explain. If someone asked me about my priorities in life, I know how I would answer. I would say it's God first (I am still searching for my definition of God), family second, and then work.

But that said, in my heart of hearts, I have always had the mindset that I would be willing to die for the greater good of mankind. Now I know that might sound strange since I just shared my priorities in life: God, family, and work, and this sounds like I am putting work before family. It is a fine line, and the best I can explain is that while work *does* come after family, work does enable me to provide for my family and give my kids a better lifestyle than I had growing up.

Therefore, if my responsibility as a medical professional requires me to lay my life on the line, as they say, it goes with the territory. This is the double-edged sword every warrior in our society must manage. I don't feel put upon that I have to make the same trade-offs, it is simply what I signed up for, and I know my fellow BORSTAR agents would all do the same things if put in a similar situation.

During the thirty-minute-plus drive toward the border, we received confirmation of a swift-water rescue situation that we needed to head directly to. We assumed that it was in the Rio Grande, but to our total shock we were told that it was on a ranch twenty miles north of the border. We were stunned, but we pressed on.

After thinking about it for a while, having been posted in this area of Texas for some time, I recalled how short, torrential rains often occurred and turned the hard-packed earth into ponds, then lakes, and then rivers. As gravity took over and the water took on a mind of its own, it came crashing toward the lowest point in the surrounding land.

We learned that there were several trucks that had been swept off the road, and that some of them had been turned over. From what we learned from the callout, it sounded like a handful of people were trapped within or on top of their trucks, and the water was still rising. We were told they had called 911 on their cell phones and sounded desperate.

What most people who don't fully understand the border don't know, is that the Border Patrol Search, Trauma, and Rescue Unit has an obligation to respond to any incident where its services are needed, not just for those involving illegal immigration. Ours is a duty to rescue persons in distress at sea, which is a core part of maritime law going back through the ages.

As we got closer to the position we were directed to, I did a quick assessment of my own personal gear, thinking about everything in my swift-water rescue bag and all the items I would need for this rescue. I like to war-game every situation, and an inventory of your gear is the first—and most vital—part of that effort.

Next is going over the goods and the bads. The goods and bads are real. Everything that can possibly happen on this mission—from a basic issue to an extreme incident—needs to be planned for. I like to play every scenario in my head so that I have already mentally prepared for it in the event it happens and can visualize a step-by-step decision-making process.

As we pulled up to our staging area, we put on our wet suits and gear and started making our way to the coordinates we were given. As much as I had tried to visualize the scene, I wasn't expecting for the water to be so high that I couldn't even recognize where we were. What used to be a ranch with high fences had now become a small, fast-moving river.

The water was up to my nipples as I and about five BORSTAR agents tiptoed through the area, trying to navigate the terrain with a few Zodiac boats. For a split second I was back in Florida-phase Ranger School, freezing my nuts off in December 2006. I would choose this challenging rescue over the known suckfest of Florida phase. Still, trying to walk as a team with a boat through heavy current over unknown debris was intimidating. During moments like this, I always think of my training, and at this moment, I realized that my training at the Academy didn't (and probably couldn't) prepare me for what a real-life swift-water rescue would actually be like.

I could hear a group of men shouting, "Over here!" and, "Hurry!" In the distance, there were four guys standing on top of a turned-over semitruck, and their feet were being covered with water. They were cold and scared. It doesn't take long for hypothermia to set in during this kind of event.

We were prepared to warm them all up in a hurry once we recovered them. I could see the relief in their eyes as we approached. I don't know what I was imagining, but these were some big burly dudes who needed our help. It was a potentially life-threatening moment, and they were showing their gratitude through smiles and hugs.

One of the bigger men gave me a hug so tight I won't ever forget it. He said in my ear: "Thank God you found us; may God bless you," in a shaking, cracking emotional voice. At that moment, I brushed it off and kept moving, but those words returned to my thoughts on the ride back home to see my kids. Regardless of your personal beliefs, when someone says that to you, it hits home and stays with you. We rescued eight people that night, and I was never prouder to be a BORSTAR agent.

After getting my feet wet with BORSTAR, literally, I was detailed to a few other missions, and some of them involved being assigned as a medic with a BORTAC team. It was my first chance to see what that side of Special Operations was all about, and I was excited to try something new and different.

During my first mission, we were laying up to try to capture a group of drug smugglers. Our intelligence unit told us that there was a strong probability of drug smuggling in the Eagle Pass area. Intel mentioned that the drug smugglers had been using this specific area at a particular time every night.

We collected that intel and created a concept of operations to interdict this group in hopes of disrupting their smuggling. It was a simple mission, but it was my first time working with BORTAC on an actual mission and not in a training exercise, and was one that had the potential to go kinetic. The BORTAC agents ran their team like a Ranger squad. I was impressed with the level of training and operational intelligence. There was a high-level tactical IQ and EQ, meaning they had a solid grasp of the operations space, similar to that of an experienced Ranger platoon with many missions under its belt.

We were working a revised midnight shift, using the night as cover and our night-vision gear to our advantage. We were transported inside of a Border Patrol Kilo Unit (the name for a specific type of Border Patrol transport truck). This unit consisted of six highly equipped dudes and a dog inside a small tin box. We hopped out of the Kilo Unit just as other Border Patrol agents made their rounds. It was business as usual.

Once the Border Patrol agent stopped his vehicle so he could look at some potential sensor activity, we snuck out the back and started making our way to our objective location. We had three possible lines of travel mapped out. We split into teams of two per location, with the dog and his handler in the middle. These types of missions often consist of a great deal of "hurry up and wait."

We planned the mission based on the intelligence we had gathered. We knew that the drug smugglers ran drugs from about 2100 to midnight. I was hoping that the dope was going to be coming my way so that our team could snag it up. Unfortunately, the smugglers didn't head my way.

The radio whispers came in: "Four packs carrying bundles wearing camouflage." My team started to slowly move closer to their area. All of a sudden, not so far away, I heard several flash bangs go off and K9 commands shouted by the dog handler. The next call on the net was: "We are Positive 46." The dog team was able to get into the fight, and we walked away with a successful mission and over four hundred pounds of dope.

The operation went extremely well and gave me a lot of confidence as a first-timer attached to BORTAC. I was excited to see what was to come on future missions. I even started to think of myself as having one foot in the door at BORSTAR and one foot in at BORTAC.

I want to take a moment to give a shout-out to a few of my fellow Border Patrol agents. These men showed real courage under the most trying, difficult, and dangerous circumstances. When people ask me today to share the highlights of my time as a Border Patrol agent, the answer is easy: It was a privilege to serve alongside men like these true professionals.

One memorable incident highlights what these heroes did. On June 15, 2013, the city of Eagle Pass, Texas, experienced severe flooding after record rainfalls. In just thirteen hours, these areas received nearly seventeen inches of rain. Many Eagle Pass residents were unaware of the dangers to come and were left stranded as floodwaters rushed through the city.

Multiple agencies were activated to respond to the flooding, including Border Patrol agents from across the Del Rio, Texas, Border Patrol Sector. Three of these agents—Rolando Cantu, James Barfield, and academy brother and BORSTAR classmate Christopher Smilo—showed tremendous courage in the face of danger, and not one hesitated to risk his own life to save another.

BORSTAR Agent Smilo was assigned to a Border Patrol airboat conducting rescue operations. He and the vessel commander, Agent Cantu, rode up and down the flooded streets of Eagle Pass looking for stranded residents. During their search, they observed what appeared to be a flashlight being waved inside a house that was nearly underwater. Agent Smilo quickly entered the fast-moving and debris-filled water to move closer to the home, where he observed two elderly occupants standing on a chair inside the house and struggling to keep their heads above the water.

Agent Smilo managed to open the front door and was immediately sucked inside by rushing waters that began to fill the rest of the home even more quickly. He regained his bearings and swam to the couple, calmly explaining that they would have to go underwater to exit the house through the front door. Though the couple was frightened, Agent Smilo's calm demeanor reassured them that he was in control of the situation and that they would be okay.

He grabbed hold of the first elderly occupant, and calmly and quickly helped her underwater, through the front door, and onto the awaiting airboat. He immediately returned to the home to retrieve the other occupant, telling the frightened man that his companion was safe and that it was his turn to exit the home. Agent Smilo then helped the man get underwater, through the front door, and onto the awaiting airboat.

As Agent Smilo was rescuing the elderly couple, Agent Cantu noticed that another elderly resident was in imminent danger of drowning. Agent Cantu maneuvered his airboat to the nearest object that he could use to secure the vessel—a telephone pole with exposed and live electrical wires. In complete disregard for his own safety, Agent Cantu secured the airboat to the pole and leapt into the water.

He swam to the frightened man's home, entered, and assured the man that everything would be all right. He then instructed the elderly gentleman to climb onto his back and wrap his arms around his neck, which gave Agent Cantu better leverage to pull the man through the open door. Agent Cantu then swam through the ever-rising, mud-filled waters to get the elderly man to safety.

In another part of town, Agent Barfield was advised of an

elderly couple stranded in an apartment complex. Despite the quickly rising floodwaters, low visibility, and dangerous road conditions, Agent Barfield responded to the call and immediately drove his Border Patrol emergency vehicle to the apartment complex. Upon arrival, Agent Barfield waded through the swift current and four-to-five-foot swells to the apartment complex to evacuate the elderly couple.

Agent Barfield met the couple at their apartment's door, but both were extremely anxious and frightened. Agent Barfield calmly explained to the couple that he would rescue them one at a time, and they both were going to be okay. He assisted the female in distress first by having her climb onto his back with her arms wrapped around his neck. He then waded through the water until he reached his vehicle and assisted her inside.

He then waded back toward the apartment, despite the fact that the floodwaters were rising and becoming even more dangerous. He assisted the husband as he had assisted the wife, and brought the man to safety. He calmly and continuously assured this elderly couple that they were going to be safe, and he risked his life to make that happen.

The events that day were devastating for the entire Eagle Pass community. While many agents assisted their fellow citizens, the actions of Agents Smilo, Cantu, and Barfield went above and beyond the call of duty. These agents never hesitated to help someone in need, knowing they were putting their own lives in danger.

By this time I had been transferred, but reading about the actions of my dear friends and their courage was inspiring. I messaged Roy Cantu after hearing about his actions that day with Smilo, and this is what he sent me:

> Tombstone courage is what I've heard it called. I heard about you stripping to your *chones* and jumping into the Rio Grande to save someone. I took that to heart. Every day since, I've never thought of myself first. I've always tried to live up to that image of you. I've had the privilege of putting on display what I would say any of my brothers would do if the moment occurred. At that moment, there's no thought other than what needs to be done. After, you think about the facts and how you could've lost your life. You think about your kids and how you hope they'd understand you did what had to be done. You recall how you weren't scared at the time, but when you think back, you realize how none of that really matters. What matters is doing the right thing at the right time. I believe we all have our moment, and my moment was the day I heard your story. I've been a better man ever since.

We never know who's watching and how our personal actions can impact others.

8

BORTAC DIRTY BIRDS

In the almost forty years since its creation in 1984, BORTAC has remained unknown to the overwhelming majority of Americans. That changed dramatically on May 24, 2022, when a crazed gunman killed twenty-one innocent people at Robb Elementary School in Uvalde, Texas. Border Patrol agents and BORTAC arrived at the school and were the ones who fatally shot the eighteen-year-old assailant.

Still, while most who followed this tragic event understood that Border Patrol agents were the ones who finally brought it to an end and likely saved many lives, the media reports did little to nothing to help the public understand what BORTAC—one of the oldest law enforcement tactical teams in the United States—is or does. I have worked with some of the most elite units in the military and some three-letter agencies, and I personally would vouch that BORTAC can match any of them. I should mention that "Dirty Birds" was the designator for the Del Rio BORTAC unit.

In order to perform their wide array of missions, BORTAC

maintains a strength of some two hundred active agents. BORTAC missions include operations against counterterrorism, drug interdiction, and threats to national security. BORTAC's core missions include direct action, foreign internal defense, special national security events, security assistance, and special reconnaissance.

Direct-action missions are short-term in nature and usually involve high-risk tactical operations, border violence, drug interdictions, and counterterrorist operations. Security-assistance missions involve performing threat assessments, protection details, and other security duties. When they perform special reconnaissance missions, BORTAC agents gather intelligence for the purposes of further identifying and stopping major violators who are involved in acts of smuggling and other criminal activities.

As described on the U.S. Customs and Border Patrol website, the Border Patrol Tactical Unit provides an immediate response capability to emergent and high-risk incidents requiring specialized skills and tactics. BORTAC has a cadre of full-time team members headquartered in El Paso, Texas, and non-full-time members dispersed throughout the United States. The teams can be called upon to deploy immediately when needed. BORTAC was initially formed to assist with disturbances—particularly riots—happening inside detention centers operated by the Immigration and Naturalization Service.

However, members of this elite tactical team no longer respond to these types of incidents. Now, BORTAC teams, operating for the Department of Homeland Security's Bureau of Customs and Border Protection, provide a global response—assisting in both national and foreign operations such as high-risk warrant service; intelligence, reconnaissance, and surveillance; foreign law enforcement; Border Patrol capacity building; air-mobile operations; and maritime operations. Notably, BORTAC agents provided support during Operation Iraqi Freedom and Operation Enduring Freedom.

BORTAC agents are regarded as one of the nation's most highly trained special operators, developing a reputation as a leading law enforcement tactical unit. The team's mission is straightforward: to respond to terrorist threats—both nationally and globally—to protect the United States homeland.

In short, BORTAC responds to incidents, threats, or potential threats not only at the U.S. Border but at many other locations. Such maneuvers have been in response to the 1987 Atlanta, Georgia, federal penitentiary riots; the 1992 Los Angeles riots; Hurricanes Katrina and Rita in 2005; and the 2015 Clinton Correctional Facility escape, just to name a few. BORTAC also undertakes "presence" missions as required at high-profile events in order to be on scene should anything untoward occur. These missions include being on-site during the 1993 World Games in Buffalo, the 2002 Winter Olympics in Salt Lake City, and Super Bowl LV in 2021 in Tampa, Florida, as well as many others. BORTAC casts a wide net internationally, and to date, its agents have operated in twenty-eight countries, assisting and training local law enforcement in areas such as border security techniques and drug enforcement tactics.

BORSTAR selection was challenging, and during that process I learned that, long-term, and for all the reasons I explained above,

I wanted to hop in with BORTAC. I was chomping at the bit. But I was still getting my footing as a BORSTAR agent. I felt like we were doing God's work, risking our lives to save others, and I was enjoying everything about it.

However, my old conversations with Staff Sergeant Barraza back in Ranger Battalion always lingered. He wanted me to be BORTAC. But I wasn't able to try out yet because the BORTAC Academy ran simultaneously to the BORSTAR selection. Therefore, I had to wait a year before applying.

While I waited, I was training and getting ready for the BORTAC selection process. BORTAC had some local missions where they needed medics attached, and BORSTAR agents were the answer. Smilo and I were the two young pups who were excited to be attached to BORTAC missions.

Up to this point there wasn't much enthusiasm in the BORSTAR ranks to join up with BORTAC. This was because BORTAC's standard operating procedure was to keep the medic in the truck until he or she was needed. Not many BORSTAR agents wanted to be benchwarmers.

However, this one SOP-driven negative wasn't the only issue. There is a long history of BORTAC and BORSTAR being like oil and water. The older version of BORSTAR was heavily focused on search and rescue. A major tasking for BORSTAR was to provide medical attention to the people attempting to cross over the U.S. border.

While we understood the importance of this mission of saving lives, there were many old-school BORTAC agents who didn't respect medics. I attribute this to the fact that they likely had never been in combat, and they didn't know the real relationship that frontline troops have with their medics. We had the utmost respect and admiration for these heroes who were willing to risk their lives to save ours.

Somehow this wasn't something the Border Patrol Special Operations agents thought much about. I think it's worth remembering that many of these old dogs joined BORTAC before the United States got involved in the war on terror after the 9/11 terrorist attacks. They were following one career path and didn't have the opportunity to serve overseas.

Therefore, it is understandable that Border Patrol Special Operations agents who didn't serve in the U.S. military post-9/11 would have no clue about the importance of medics in a hostile encounter. Believe me, I had some heated discussions with BORTAC agents on this topic, and some old dogs were adamant that they would never change their views. Luckily that generation has slowly retired, and a new wave of leadership has since been involved in missions that required a medic's expertise.

As I mentioned earlier, the SOP for BORTAC missions was to have the BORSTAR agent stay "on call" in a staging vehicle for when he or she was needed. This made no sense to me, and I was frustrated and angry that my fellow Border Patrol agents were so obstinate about this point. As I said earlier, oil and water.

One day, as we were going through a lengthy pre-mission briefing, when it was my time to talk about the emergency medical plan for the operations, I recommended attaching a BORSTAR medic to the team directly on the "X," which is a term we use for the objective location. One of the BORTAC agents replied: "It's not safe to have a medic with us in case there is contact." Contact on a border isn't likely but is definitely possible. "Contact" in the tactical world isn't a literal term as in touch and feel, but is a reference to "troops in contact" in a shooting engagement.

I stood up out of frustration that had been building inside me for the past few months. I asked: "How many guys on the team have combat experience?" The room was quiet. One BORTAC agent raised his hand. I had more combat experience as a trigger-puller than the whole team. I wasn't trying to be a smart-ass, but I had to get it through their thick BORTAC brains that I was an asset, not a liability. They all knew my background, and I didn't have to explain my point of view any further.

They finally supported my recommendation and placed me on the X with the rest of the team. On the night of the operation there was a pack of wild pigs gathered directly in a path that would lead us to the high-point position we were trying to get to. The situation was dire. It was a time-sensitive situation based on the intel. The illegal traffic that we were trying to get a visual on was getting closer, and we had an obstacle in the way. This wasn't the first time I had dealt with wild pigs, and I was prepared for this exact moment. I pulled out an unauthorized slingshot with a ball bearing and let it rip. The attempt was successful. During this mission we were able to get ourselves into a high-point location that enabled us to discover the group of smugglers. This situation was eerily reminiscent of my combat tour in Mosul, Iraq, and a rock toss with Staff Sergeant Barraza.

Once we were able to convince BORTAC agents of the value

of BORSTAR medics, our experience working directly with BORTAC became more successful. In the summer of that year 2013, I was pulled in for a three-month detail to Rio Grande Valley Sector near McAllen, Texas. We packed our gear and headed to work. The housing that we were staying in was an older military barracks on the outskirts of the city. The buildings were similar to hunting cabins.

As soon as we got to town we were given our assignment. We were asked to surveil this sector in numbers because the area was being overwhelmed by illegal immigrants, as well as a massive influx of drug smugglers who were evading the limited number of Border Patrol agents. Our mission was to provide extra support to the local BORTAC teams.

One of the first operations we conducted was a reconnaissance of Lake Falcon. This is an international reservoir on the Rio Grande forty miles southeast of Laredo, Texas, that touches Nuevo Laredo, Tamaulipas, Mexico. Due to the fact that it straddles the border, it is a well-known location for drug smuggling. It is also a dangerous area. In 2012, a U.S. citizen, David Hartley, was murdered at Lake Falcon, and his death was traced to a ruthless drug trafficking organization.

We were dressed like everyday fishermen, but we had loaded full battle rattle gear (a term used to describe full tactical mission essential items) with a medical bag at the foot of our boat in the event that, while pulling recon of the area, something might pop off. It was one of those "hope nothing happens" moments so we could actually use the fishing gear we brought as part of our cover.

The only issue was the fact that I had never officially gone fishing. The closest I came was when I used a can wrapped in fishing line to try and snag a catfish in the Rio Grande river in Canutillo, Texas, with my Tío Roy (*tío* is Spanish for "uncle"). My only other fishing experience was when I took my young kids to a catch-and-release pond. We used hot dogs for bait, and the kids had Spider-Man and Barbie fishing poles.

With that modest "background" as a fisherman, I was now on an operation pretending to be experienced enough to have made a journey to Lake Falcon to catch fish. And during this dead time, we really *did* want to catch some fish. I had my line in the water and wanted to catch a fish *now*. My boys, Donny and Felix and my supervisor, Pete Sanchez, were experienced fishermen and were laughing at my ineptitude and impatience. I wasn't raised doing things like this. The only versions of hunting and fishing and camping that I knew about were what the Army taught me, and I don't want anything to do with that version of it.

About three hours into this game of casting and reeling, looking for a honey hole, I got a bite! Everyone else in the boat yelled: "Hook it, hook it!" I pulled as hard as I could and hooked a fish. It was so wild. I just kept reeling it in, and eventually, a nice-looking bass came out the water. It was my first fish.

That night we went back to our campsite and cooked the fish we had caught—a few catfish and my decent-sized bass. I gutted it, descaled it, seasoned it, grilled it, and ate it. On one of my last bites a bone punctured the back of my throat and about killed me. The largemouth bass got the last laugh, and the operation as a whole didn't generate any new evidence.

I am mindful that this is my story and that most memories involve only the man or woman telling their story to readers. That said, BORTAC is such an important national asset that I wanted to share the stories of two of my BORTAC comrades. Due to OPSEC (operations security is a security and risk management process and strategy that classifies information, and then determines what is required to protect sensitive information and prevent it from getting into the wrong hands) reasons, I am not at liberty to reveal their names, but I assure you that they both served with honor. These two gentlemen embody all that is great about the Border Patrol in general and BORTAC in particular. Here are their stories:

BORTAC 1:

In my law enforcement career, I had the privilege of working alongside a few men who had served in combat in Ranger Battalion. To a man, these guys were top-notch operators who quickly mastered their environment, adapted to threats, and executed with precision and effectiveness. I'm a former Marine, but have never served in combat. My Ranger buddies didn't care. They viewed me as a brother in arms, and it was my honor to wear a badge and gun alongside them as we defended the rule of law stateside under a civilian chain of command.

I worked for the Border Patrol for eight years; six of those as a BORTAC Operator. BORTAC is an abbreviation for Border Patrol Tactical Unit. The easiest way to describe it to people outside the community is to call it the SWAT team for the Border Patrol, but that is a simplification worthy only of passing conversation. My work as a BORTAC agent was extremely broad and included warrant service, high-risk field interdiction, covert surveillance operations, HVT operations, antiterrorism ruse operations, and riverine ops. One week, work might entail wearing a wet suit and swim fins. The next might see my team serving an FBI warrant or lying in wait on a dope trail for armed drug mules. For the men who worked on those teams, variety was part of the draw. The unique work environment attracted veterans to try out for the teams, and at the time of my service, we were vet heavy. It made me feel at home.

While BORTAC handled the tactical operations side of Border Patrol Special Operations, another team, BORSTAR, took care of the medical and rescue aspects of high-risk endeavors. Those agents maintained a seemingly endless list of certifications: tactical medic, rescue diver, high-angle rescue, HRST master, and swift-water specialist were just a few. There was no environment along the border where they could not operate, bringing with them the highest level of competence and professionalism. Knowing there was a BORSTAR medic nearby was a great source of comfort to any BORTAC team.

The evolution of BORTAC operations was and is on-going. The border is anything but a static environment and requires unending adjustment to the constantly changing tactics of the various cartels and human/narcotics smuggling organizations operating in Northern Mexico. At one point during my service, each BORTAC team was assigned a BORSTAR medic as a fully operational member of the team. The medic had to volunteer for this duty and worked and trained alongside the team as a full member. This caused a little heartburn among some of the old-school BORTACers, but I liked the idea. Having a real medic on the team trained in more than the standard gunshot wound care was a big force multiplier. In addition, the medic was a volunteer. BORTAC operations boiled down to dirty work done in the dark. Anyone who volunteered for a team billet knew what he was in for, so those volunteers tended to be guys already comfortable with being uncomfortable.

The value of the volunteer medic was more than just medical, it could be tactical too. Our medic was Vince Vargas, a former Ranger with a big personality and experience to match. He was not shy about wanting to be in the thick of any action and was uniquely prepared for the unexpected in ways we would soon come to appreciate.

One night, my team was headed to the river to lay in on a trail that had seen recent dope-smuggling activity. A camera had captured an image of a drug scout in the area carrying a revolver, so we were anticipating a good night. Leaving the operational details out, the general plan was to insert away from the river and ruck in to a predetermined location where we'd set up along a trail and wait for contact. On the way in, we encountered a group of wild pigs. Animals, wild or domestic, in the AO are generally not a good thing due to their tendency to give away a position. (As a sniper, I once had to pepper spray a horse that got too close to my hide site.) The patrol halted as we tried to figure out how best to get the pigs out of the area without driving them closer to the river and possibly giving up our location. Intervals on an LE patrol aren't as long as they are in the military, partly due to the heavy brush and partly due to the size of the patrol—a lower number of operators means fewer guys to get on line in the event of contact, so distance is typically shorter, plus the threat of indirect fire is nonexistent. But I digress.

Because of our close proximity, Vince was quickly apprised of the situation and immediately responded with a characteristic grin. "I got it," he said, and dropped his ruck. Unbeknownst to us, Vince had dealt with lots of position-compromising dogs during his deployments to Iraq and automatically included his cure to this ill in his standard loadout—an old-school wrist rocket slingshot and a handful of steel ball bearings. We started laughing our asses off—as quietly as possible—while Vince loaded up a ball bearing and took aim at the nearest pig, maybe twenty-five yards out. He bounced one off the pig's backside with what seemed like well-honed accuracy. A couple of additional well-placed thumps later and the pigs headed north away from the river, and the mission continued. Silence is mission critical for tactical border operations, and Vince had pulled off a save in complete silence with an implement that not one of us would have thought to bring. Everyone on that patrol learned something that day from a Ranger who showed up prepared for a problem no one else anticipated, but that could have easily compromised the op.

I miss the Border Patrol. I miss the geography of the border. I miss the work. But most of all, I miss the guys: problem solvers like Vince who always found a way to dominate a situation, learn from it, and laugh along the way.

So again, we were working in Rio Grande Valley, and there were four of us in a vehicle. A local guy and our supervisor were in the front, and Vince and I were in the back. We were communicating with an air asset that had eyes on a vehicle that just dropped off a load of narcotics. The air asset guided us to the vehicle. We pulled up behind it and turned on our emergency lights. The vehicle hesitated for a few moments, as if contemplating if it was going to take off or pull over. We were chattering and discussing what we were going to do with the vehicle. The vehicle eventually pulled over on an incredibly busy highway.

The command was given to extract the driver out of the vehicle before it took off. Vince and our driver were the closest and were the biggest guys. They bolted to the vehicle as I came up from the passenger side, holding a position and keeping eyes on the other passenger in the vehicle. The poor driver was thinking that he got pulled over by the average agent, but unbeknownst to him Vince and our driver were massive guys and moved with purpose.

I watched them pull this guy out of the driver side window while vehicles were streaming by us and honking. This guy was parallel to the ground and probably five feet or so in the air. His eyes were panicked as he realized this was definitely not the average agents' protocol. He was taken to the ground and handcuffed quickly. I will always remember and laugh at that dude's face. A bit of his manhood was taken that night. Vince and our driver owned him.

BORTAC 2:
Our BORTAC team was detailed down to the Rio Grande Valley Sector. This sector was the busiest in the Border Patrol at this time. We were working at the busiest station, in the busiest sector. In particular, we were working the busiest zone in all of the Border Patrol. Large volumes of narcotics were coming through the area.

We were working with the local BORTAC team.

One night we were able to follow a load vehicle to a house, I don't recall if we used an air asset or not, but nonetheless we had the narcotics at the house. Calls were made to get approval from higher headquarters in order to hit the house. We staged nearby and finally got the approval we needed.

The subjects were called out and detained. Our team quickly entered the house. This place was a nice residence and was a decent size. There were separate basement living quarters for one of the guys we arrested. I remember clearing the room and admiring his artwork. He had a large framed picture of him and his girlfriend. It was very reminiscent of something Pablo Escobar would do, but this was lower budget and in a basement room.

We continued to clear the house without incident. We found some guns and other contraband. Our team gathered in the garage, getting status checks and making sure we hadn't overlooked anything. One of the guys looked up and saw an attic door. The roof was peaked, so there was ample space to hide things that the occupants didn't want to be found.

Two of our guys volunteered to go up into the attic. One covered the other as the smaller of the two rummaged around the attic. We were in a half circle waiting for the attic dwellers to give us the word of anything. One of the attic guys tried to move his position but missed a crossbeam, and sheetrock started to crack.

This caused him to take a corrective to step onto another crossbeam, but he missed that one also.

I was watching this unfold. His boots were now visible as sheet rock cascaded down. Suddenly, I saw Vince (I never knew him as Rocco) run under the attic dweller. His arms were outstretched, and he was yelling, "I got you," or something very similar to that. I smiled, enjoying the fact that Vince, knowing full well there was no chance he was going to catch someone from ten feet up, weighing about 210–220 pounds with all his gear. This was exactly what I wanted out of my medic. The attic dweller never fell, but he did leave a nice hole in the ceiling, and he was ridiculed unmercifully when it was all over. My takeaway was this: Vince was my medic and that's a good thing.

As I explained at the outset, and as these gentlemen have described above, given the desperation of those migrants trying to cross the border, as well as the criminals—coyotes and drug smugglers—who will stop at nothing to keep their extremely lucrative businesses alive, BORTAC is needed more today than it has ever been.

It is worth explaining that the Special Operations teams have access to a wide array of special equipment and other assets that enable them to take on even the most challenging missions. As a newbie attached to BORTAC, I felt that the Border Patrol leadership was giving us everything that we needed to succeed.

Here is how I recall one of the missions my buddy talked about.

I was on detail to McAllen with my team again in 2013. My supervisor during this three-month stretch was a former military officer, Beau Baggot. He had a great deal of combat experience as well as incredible poise. His strong accent was a mix, kind of Texan and kind of Southern. He had a tactical swagger about him, and I loved the way he looked at an objective. He was 100 percent an outside-the-box thinker in everything we did. I have grown to love guys like this; they make this job exciting and interesting.

For example, one night we headed out to a high point to observe the river and look for drug traffickers. He walked up to us to give us the current status of the operation. "Hey fellas, looks like this mission is a go." Then he paused and began to tell us about his new shoes. "You know what, after all these years wearing god-awful military-style boots, I've decided to just start wearing my Chuck Taylors on missions."

He cracked us all up with random comments like that, all designed, no doubt, to relieve the tension we felt when we were about to embark on a potentially dangerous mission. Comments like that are why I would always work for this man.

That night, somehow, he was able to convince an air asset (that I am not at liberty to name) to take a few spins in our area of operations. We waited at our location for word from the eyes in the sky. During this time, our normal Border Patrol–issued radios were compromised; several of our Border Patrol vehicles had been broken into, and some of our radios had been cloned.

Since this was an important operation, we opted to use our cell phones and communicate via text message. This was a first for me, but knowing the situation, I wasn't upset about it.

> Alright, gents, we got ourselves some dope. We are going to follow the vehicle to its drop point, and let it load up. Y'all get to your trucks, and stand by for more information.

We loaded up with some local BORTACers and waited for further information. The drug-loaded vehicle that we were focused on was headed to a drop-off location. They had no idea we had eyes on the load vehicle and were following it to its final destination.

The vehicle pulled up to a house and went around back to park. Still, the team sat back and waited for the word. The dope was dropped off and the driver left the house.

The vehicle that my team was following pulled into a Red Barn, a local chain drive-through liquor store.

We were assigned to take that vehicle down, while the other two teams were simultaneously headed to take down the house.

The air asset guided us to the target vehicle. They pulled into the Red Barn, and we had to decide about when to jump the vehicle. I was in the back seat on the driver's side, and a local BORTACer named Q was the driver. Each of us could pass for a defensive end in an amateur Mexican football league. The vehicle pulled out of the Red Barn parking lot, and the air asset lit them up with an IR (infrared) beam to positively identify the correct vehicle in the middle of rush hour.

The order came for us on the ground to light them up as well. We hit the vehicle with lights and sirens, and as soon as they pulled over, Q and I pushed out and moved to the vehicle with our rifles at the ready. As we approached from the driver's side, we saw that his window was lowered and his hands were clear and didn't have a weapon. We pulled him out the window as fast as we could. Having two 250-pound dudes pull out a 100-pound dope smuggler is almost comical; however, it almost ended catastrophically. As we pulled him out to lay him down in the street to cuff him, a vehicle was quickly approaching. Luckily, we snatched him back toward us before any of us was hit.

The smuggler and vehicle were now in custody, and it was time to meet with the other team to see if they needed any assistance. We returned to the house, and the scene we found there was straight from the movies. The building was surrounded by surveillance cameras, and the house was filled with fancy decorations and half-nude paintings of what I assumed was the wife of the homeowner. I don't know who lived there or what the owner was associated with, but he was definitely making a lot more money than the average person based on the cars, house, and expensive items he had lying around. This was an extremely successful mission. It's not common when catching dope bundles that you can attach the driver, the vehicle, and the drop house to the case.

This would be the deployment that gave birth to my nickname, "Big Papi." There was a BORTACer named Kevin Vichini that the team called "Big Papa." I have no idea about the origination of the name—maybe it was because he was a large muscular operator—but once I got used to it, we became close. We would work out together and drink a few beers together and talk shit. It was like a brotherly friendship. Since we spent so much time together, our teammate, Donny, started calling me "Big Papi," which is the Hispanic version of Kevin's nickname. Once that name stuck, I kept referencing it when talking about myself.

While on that same detail in McAllen, Texas, we had the mission to disrupt the local drug trafficking operations in the area. At the time, it was the busiest sector in the nation. Sadly for the almost half million residents of McAllen and the surrounding cities of Brownsville and Edinburg, this area is central for drugs coming across our southern border.

On this particular mission, we had been laying up in an agricultural field for several nights, and on each night we had no movement. This isn't uncommon. Sometimes, the traffic patterns change or our efforts become compromised. We had changed the infiltration vehicle every night, and we adjusted our infil and exfil routes each time we dismounted. We made every effort to create a thriving environment in an unpredictable climate. But if you spend every night lying in the dark for hours, it can be difficult to stay focused.

Pete Sanchez was the supervisor on this trip, and he was very laid back. He was highly proficient at his job as a supervisor and wasn't the micromanager type. My partners to the left and right were Kevin, Felix, Donny, and Brock.

It is hard to prepare for this type of engagement. Drug trafficking criminals have a reputation for being armed during these types of transports. Just a month before our arrival in McAllen, in this exact location, there was an exchange of rounds between BORTAC and some drug smugglers. No one was injured, and the smugglers absconded to Mexico.

I was thinking about basic firefight tactics like cover and concealment. We were sitting ducks in this open area where crops had been recently harvested. Our only advantage was the dark. There was almost no light. We knew that the traffickers couldn't see us unless we were five feet from them. We were about fifty yards from the cane, and the river was only five yards from there.

We were anticipating that the smugglers would carry the bundles on the road to the left or right of us. But as luck would have it, they sent a scout ahead to scope the area before they made their way to the drop-off point.

I saw the scout and mentioned it to the team. We weren't sure what would be best, to rush them and potentially spook them or wait for them to come to us.

We decided to push forward and jump the group by the river landing. We crept closer and closer, and as we got to within a few yards of them, they started loading the bundles on each other's backs. We didn't have much time.

I knew it was now or never, so I decided to jump the group.

I ran to the closest mule, but at this point, they heard us running with all our gear, and noise-light discipline was out the window. *"PARATE!"* I yelled.

They dumped the dope and ran back to the river. The individual I was locked in on just pulled back into the cane to where I couldn't see him anymore. I had no idea what was past the cane, but I was willing to risk it since if we catch dope without a body, there is no case. All of our hard work would be wasted.

I jumped through the cane as fast as I could—it was a complete "here goes nothing" attempt. I was lucky enough to catch his heels so that he tripped and landed face-first. We scrambled, and I got up first to control him and put him in cuffs.

We snagged three of the six who were attempting to smuggle six hundred pounds of dope. The operation was successful, and we disrupted this smuggling attempt for the night.

There are so many more stories to tell about my time in McAllen and being attached to the Del Rio BORTAC team, the "Dirty Birds." It was fun while it lasted, and we were able to disrupt some smuggling organizations during my time there.

Shortly after my redeployment to Del Rio, I received an email stating that the Border Patrol SOG (Special Operations Group) had an available position, and I was eligible to apply. The dream of becoming an SOG operator was in my sights.

9

BORDER PATROL SPECIAL OPERATIONS GROUP

In 2007, the U.S. Border Patrol joined together two units, the Border Patrol Tactical Unit (BORTAC) and the Border Patrol Search, Trauma, and Rescue Unit (BORSTAR), to form the U.S. Border Patrol's Special Operations Group (SOG), headquartered in El Paso, Texas. BORTAC and BORSTAR direct their nationally dispersed assets from SOG, providing the U.S. Border Patrol with immediate tactical and emergency response assets.

SOG provides the Department of Homeland Security (DHS), U.S. Customs and Border Protection (CBP), and the U.S. Border Patrol with specially trained and equipped teams capable of rapid response to emergent and uncommon law enforcement situations requiring special tactics and techniques, search and rescue, and medical response capabilities.

BORTAC and BORSTAR advance the missions of the Border Patrol and U.S. Customs and Border Protection CBP by handling uncommon and dangerous situations outside the normal scope of Border Patrol agent duties. BORTAC and BORSTAR accomplish their goals through planning and training. SOG deploys to domestic and international intelligence-driven and antiterrorism efforts as well as to disaster and humanitarian special operations.

SOG's in-house Intelligence Unit (SOG IU) provides vital mission-critical field intelligence to SOG assets. SOG IU conducts electronic targeting and collections and provides additional support for selected CBP missions and Border Patrol sector intelligence initiatives.

The command staff for the Mobile Response Team (MRT) is also located at SOG Headquarters. SOG provides the MRT, which is a rapidly deployable asset capable of addressing problematic areas along the nation's borders, with training, equipment, and logistical support.

As a highly mobile rapid-response tool, SOG significantly increases the ability of the DHS, CBP, and the U.S. Border Patrol to respond operationally to specific terrorist threats and incidents, as well as to support traditional Border Patrol operations.

I have always known my goal was to become an SOG agent; I just didn't know how to do that. From what I'd read about them, they were the top tier of the Border Patrol, and that's what I wanted for myself and for the memory of Staff Sergeant Barraza. I also wanted to prove that I was still good enough to be part of the Border Patrol's most elite unit.

By this time, in late 2013, I was training to try out for BORTAC. Unfortunately, it was a rough time in my life. I was going through a difficult divorce, and to add to it I became the custodial parent for my four kids. Nonetheless, I was able to maintain enough focus to still be good at my job and to try to find a way to get to SOG.

While I was at the Border Patrol Academy, one of the senior medics who heard about my background approached me. He thought I would be a great asset to the BORSTAR team and that I needed to ensure I got through the selection process. His message inspired me to stay the course and focus on trying out for that elite unit.

By this time, I had already instructed the next BORSTAR class and made a name for myself. I had led classes as a drill sergeant and felt very comfortable in the role of class moderator, a similar position to that of a senior drill sergeant. It was all about maintaining the order of the course and serving as a conduit between cadre and students. I had also, with the help of several others, implemented tactical medicine in the Academy and introduced patrolling.

Patrolling is a military tactic. Small groups or individual units are deployed from a larger formation to achieve a specific objective and then return. The tactic of patrolling may be applied to ground troops, armored units, naval units, and combat aircraft.

BORSTAR was already teaching and training with TAC-MED (tactical medicine), which most military personnel referred to as Tactical Combat Casualty Care (TCCC). However, what BORSTAR as a whole missed when teaching tactical medicine was that they needed to teach the basics of patrolling as well. I felt that unless they did that, they weren't bridging the gap between

BORSTAR tactical medics and BORTAC. The two units would still be like oil and water.

I wanted to be part of the solution, so I applied for a lateral transfer to the SOG. There was a long list of agents who had put in for this position. I knew most had been in BORSTAR longer than I had, but I believed I had an edge because of my military Special Operations experience. In addition, I knew several members of the "top brass" in BORSTAR who wanted to make some serious strides in tactical medicine and who knew that I could help facilitate that effort. I knew that if this all happened, I would get a lateral transfer to El Paso, Texas, with the SOG.

I got the job, packed up the kids, and headed west. I was specifically asked to come teach as part of the BORSTAR selection cadre, and specifically to be the SME (subject matter expert) for the TAC-MED program.

Because I was still getting my footing as the custodial parent for my kids, I asked to be a part of the training team until I could get them situated. I spent a better part of two years running the BORSTAR selection process and training the Mobile Response Teams (MRT) across the border.

The Mobile Response Teams are a different beast. The MRT mission is to provide a national group of organized, trained, and equipped Border Patrol agents who are capable of rapid movement to regional and national incidents in support of priority U.S. Customs and Border Protection operations. MRT supports a flexible and enhanced tiered response capability to counter the emerging, changing, and evolving threats in the most challenging operational areas along our nation's borders. MRT provides the mobilization assets to vulnerable border areas by augmenting the number of agents to mitigate gaps in operational control of the border and non-border areas as ordered.

MRT was created to provide the Border Patrol with a rapidly deployable asset that can address high-threat areas along the nation's borders and other regions of the United States as ordered. MRT is available to respond to regional and national incidents in support of U.S. Customs and Border Protection operations. Currently, there are eleven participating sectors: San Diego, Tucson, El Paso, Laredo, Rio Grande Valley, Detroit, Spokane, Houlton, Swanton, Blaine, and Buffalo.

Some MRT accomplishments during 2021 include a deployment to the 2021 Presidential Inauguration in January to support U.S. Secret Service protective operations and, in March, its first out-of-the-country training in Panama City, Panama. The latter deployment trained local law enforcement officers in crowd control techniques. There are currently 484 active MRT agents nationwide, divided among eleven sectors, including SOG.

I started traveling with a training unit that taught other BORTAC and BORSTAR sectors and recertified them in their TAC-MED procedures. I was also attempting to implement a new force training curriculum based on the Army Combatives Program. I brought on Matt Larsen who was known as the founder and creator of the Modern Army Combatives Program (MACP) to help develop something that would be more effective and focused on weapons retention. We taught four courses with no injuries. However, I couldn't get the Border Patrol to support any additional courses.

While I feel quite confident in my ability to train colleagues in the use of force, I think it is worth explaining why I brought in Matt Larsen. Bringing in outside talent like Matt to help make agents better prepared to do their jobs in a high-stress, kinetic, and potentially deadly situation was, in my judgment, just flat-out the right thing to do.

In 2001, Matt Larsen, then a sergeant first class, established the United States Army Combatives School at Fort Benning, Georgia. Students are taught techniques from the 2002 and 2009 versions of FM 3–25.150 (Combatives), also written by Larsen. The aim of the regimen is to teach soldiers how to train rather than giving them the perfect techniques for any given situation. The main idea is that all real ability is developed after the initial training and only if that training becomes routine.

The initial techniques simply serve as a useful learning metaphor for teaching important concepts, such as dominating an opponent with superior body position during ground grappling or controlling someone during clinch fighting. These techniques are taught as simple, easily repeatable drills, in which practitioners rapidly learn multiple related techniques. For example, Drill One teaches the following: escaping blows, maintaining the mount, escaping the mount, maintaining the guard, passing the guard, assuming side control, maintaining side control, and preventing and assuming the mount. The drill can be completed in less than a minute and can be done repeatedly with varying levels of resistance to maximize training benefits.

New soldiers begin their combatives training on day three of initial military training, when they are first issued their rifle.

The training begins with learning to maintain control of one's weapon in a fight. Soldiers are then taught how to gain control of a potential enemy at the farthest possible range to maintain their tactical flexibility, what the tactical options are, and how to implement them.

The three basic options taught as possible reactions to encountering a resistant opponent are: (1) disengage to regain projectile weapon range; (2) gain a controlling position and utilize a secondary weapon; (3) close the distance and gain control to finish the fight.

You can see how important it was to have Matt Larsen along as a true subject matter expert who was ready, willing, and able to help my fellow Border Patrol agents survive in a fight with a determined coyote, drug smuggler, or even frightened illegal immigrant. Any of these could easily decide to fight it out with the Border Patrol agent trying to apprehend them rather than be taken into custody.

I had been in this role for some time, and while I felt that I *was* making an impact, I was becoming bored in the training department at SOG. I felt I had reached the limit of how I could impact the program and that it was time to move on. I also missed the fight by not being in the field. Even more, I missed being on a team with a mission to execute.

If I was going to jump onto a BORTAC team as a medic, I would be willing to work only for Chris Voss. Chris was a dual tabber: BORSTAR and BORTAC. He had an extensive background as a combat-experienced Ranger and many years on the teams.

Voss was "the standard," and I would be honored to serve alongside a Ranger in BORTAC. I mentioned to Voss that I was interested in getting back in the field, and I would love to bring my experience to the team. Our military careers had meshed— some of his friends from his time in the military were later in charge of me during my time. We often talked about them and what they were currently doing. We also had some serious conversations about how BORSTAR could be a bigger asset to the team and how I could be implemented into his group.

He was excited to pull me into his team, but approval had to come through the chain of command. I had to do an informal interview with Special Operations Supervisor (SOS) Larimore. The interview went well. Once I got permission to attach with BORTAC, the leadership pulled me into their training like I was one of their own. Voss mentioned: "I know you are our medic, but I am going to treat you as I do anyone else on my team."

Voss's Ranger background made me feel comfortable, and we got along well right away. He had me shooting live fires with the team on day one. I knew the standard operating procedures (SOPs) were the same as they were in Ranger Battalion. BORTAC agents clear rooms the same way we had done in Iraq and Afghanistan, but with different methods of breaching.

During such a training event, we pulled up to the shoot house. It was a familiar place and quite similar to the training environment in Ranger Battalion. They put me in the stack as if I was a BORTACer myself. I appreciated the confidence, but I was nervous because I thought I would be rusty.

We entered the front door and immediately saw an open

door on the right side that we flowed into. I was number three man in the order of movement. We entered the room, and immediately the number one and number two men engaged the threat. I was well within my rights to shoot too, but I hesitated and decided not to.

The overpressure from the rifles and the smell of gunpowder hit me with a wave of memories, and in that moment of hesitation, I told myself: "You remember." I remembered why I love this stuff. I remembered the countless repetitions in Battalion. Slow is smooth and smooth is fast. I remembered SSG Barraza's methods of training and all my years of kicking in doors. We exited the room and flowed out into the hallway, where another threat popped up. However, the number one man's weapon went cold due to a malfunction, and I was now the number two man.

As the number one stepped slightly left to clear the way, I covered down on the shot and let a controlled pair loose to hit the target. I stepped in front and followed the threat into the room with the rest of the team behind me. It was just like riding a bike, just a reaction; I didn't have to think. I didn't even realize what I had done until we finished clearing the house. The range supervisor pulled me to the side and asked about my background. I told him, and he just smirked. It was the vote of approval that I needed.

I was now attached as a medic to the number one BORTAC SOG Team, ready to deploy anywhere in the world at a moment's notice.

A few months later, we were deployed for a training mission to improve our team's standard operating procedures. Especially with me now being on the team, we needed to make sure we were working as a cohesive unit and always sharpening our skills. Unbeknownst to us, we were running hostage rescue training missions in Quantico with other agencies. After that week of running many iterations, moving as a tactical unit by land and by air assault, I was confident that this team was ready.

SOG can be deployed anywhere in the world that our services are needed. There were times that we were briefed on potential missions that I had never imagined the DHS would be involved in. These included, for example, helping other countries devise plans to fortify their borders, as well as improve their tactical medicine training. I had grown my beard out for some missions, and for others I had worn plain clothes.

I never made the time to try out for BORTAC myself. I was too inundated with the kids and being attached to SOG. Somehow, life seemed to keep pulling me in different directions. I was proud to have finally achieved the level of expertise and proficiency I had set out to accomplish. I did this not only for myself but for the memory of Staff Sergeant Ricardo Barraza. A big part of me felt like I was making him proud by living out his dream. I had reached the top of my game, and all I had left to do was to be the best medic I could be for my comrades.

10

ESCAPE AND MANHUNT

We were at the command center in Dannemora, New York, home of the Clinton Correctional Facility, also called Dannemora after the town. One of the local law enforcement officials told us that this prison had once served as a massive insane asylum and was named Dannemora State Hospital for the Criminally Insane. I remember thinking: "How appropriate."

We received a briefing that was essentially the same as what we heard back in Texas at our headquarters. Two inmates, Richard Matt and David Sweat—both incarcerated for murder—were discovered missing during an early morning bed check. Matt was serving twenty-five years to life, and Sweat was serving life without parole. The two prisoners had dug a tunnel out of the prison with tools obtained from a prison employee.

The town of Dannemora was on high alert; everyone was looking for Matt and Sweat. The "intelligence" was rolling in, but as is the case in many situations like this, most of the information we received consisted of false alarms.

Some of the law enforcement officials at the command center heard the words "Border Patrol" and didn't understand why we were there in the first place. We had to explain how we were trained and that we had a great deal of experience in tracking people. The first bit of intelligence suggested that Matt and Sweat might be headed to the southern border. Later, we realized the distance to Mexico would be nearly impossible to cover on foot, so our collective determination was that they were headed north.

Our first mission was on an island, where a small fishing cabin showed signs that someone had broken in. It was determined that the best method of insertion would be on motorboats, and the geography of the island was such that there was enough cover surrounding the cabin and we could approach without undue risk.

As the medic, I always try to consider every threat that can impact my team. And on this mission, all I could think about was the insertion phase, and how our team hadn't had much familiarity with this method of closing in on a target via waterborne craft. The closest thing I had experienced that even vaguely resembled a water mission was flying over the Tigris River in Iraq.

I had a quick talk with the boys before the mission. I reminded them how heavy we were with our tactical gear on, and that they should jettison all their gear as soon as possible if they fell into the water. I was the poster child for wanting to avoid falling into the water. At the time, I was about 245 pounds, and with "full battle rattle" gear I was at 315 pounds, maybe more with my med bag attached.

We split the teams and took two boats. I was on the first boat with Voss, Cavazos, and Pitts. We created a 360 perimeter (360 degrees of security), knowing that two dangerous escaped convicts could be less than one hundred meters away. Once the rest of the team disembarked from the boats, we got into the order of movement and started to patrol toward the potential objective.

Our tactics were similar to that of an Army infantry platoon, which consists of seven or eight troops patrolling terrain. We walked through the thick vegetation of the island but had almost no visual of the target. This was the real thing, and a million thoughts surged through my mind. *Be ready; this could be it—head on a swivel.*

While I tried to compartmentalize, the mission brought flashbacks to my time Iraq, the only difference being the rules of engagement. Also, besides Voss and a former Marine on the team (whose name I will not mention for privacy reasons), I was the only other guy who had been in real-life tactical engagements. Not that BORTAC members weren't capable and highly trained. I just felt that I needed to stay close to Voss on the approach. Knowing he took point, I wanted to be the second man into the house behind him.

I heard the command: "Open door front!" For our SOP for this operation, we flowed into the house, pieing corners and clearing the small cabin in a few seconds. "Dry hole" is a term used in Ranger Battalion for an empty objective. The targets were not there and, from the look of it, maybe never were. It could have just been a coincidence that the cabin was suspicious, or maybe Matt and Sweat *did* break in to steal what they needed and continued moving.

We returned to the operations command center and prepared for the next set of orders. There was some solid information that the two escaped convicts were squatting at an old, abandoned school. It was quite a distance way, so we had to take Black Hawk helicopters (which, I believe, were owned by the National Guard) to reach the school. We received the mission brief and created two chalks (a chalk is a flight assignment or manifest that identifies which bird you will be traveling in) and loaded up the aircraft. It was about a twenty-minute flight to the objective area.

There is a now-infamous photo taken by Special Operations Supervisor Larimore of "BORTAC" on a Black Hawk headed to the objective area to open a can of whoop-ass on Matt and Sweat that has circulated on the internet. If you look closely enough, you will see me, Big Papi, in the back-right door of the Black Hawk with my feet dangling out the bird. I had a reflective flag on my bump helmet that I liked because it was similar to the ones we wore overseas on my first deployment with Ranger Battalion. On the other side of the helmet was a "Dirty Bird" Velcro patch. This was a tip of the cap to my original sector, Del Rio SOD (Special Operations Detachment).

On missions like these, there is calm before the storm. The boat ride to the island was the calm before the storm of that mission. Then, the only worry that I had during the boat operations was that my guys wouldn't fall into the water by overcompensating their weight on a boat. (In full tactical load, operators have a high potential to be top-heavy and any slight adjustment on a boat could cause it to capsize.) But this mission, this air assault was different. We weren't in combat, and I wasn't worried about the typical issues, such as RPG attacks, that I usually thought about before a mission back in my Army days. So I was taking in the fresh air that only people who have sat on the steel deck of a military helicopter have experienced—fresh air mixed with JP8 fumes blasted into your lungs. That scent always fired me up for a mission.

I took a minute to soak it all in. I smiled and laughed to myself. I stuck my arm out of the bird and moved it in an up-and-down motion like I used to do as a kid in the passenger seat of my father's truck. In moments like these, you feel free. Truth be told, I wasn't thinking about the birthday party for my daughter that I was about to miss. I wasn't thinking about the potential of catching a bullet in the face as soon as we landed. I wasn't thinking about anything but this moment and this smell. It was my version of peace.

My thoughts were broken by the voice coming over the intercom: "Ten minutes!" The radio chatter began to intensify. The moments of calm and peace I was having turned, with the flip of a switch, into battle readiness. I began war-gaming this mission, what-iffing every possible scenario, and asking myself what could possibly happen. Being left-handed, I had to always be cautious of bumping my mag release with my bulky gear and magazine pouches on the front of my rig. I thought about all of the possible options that could happen on dismount during a live objective and every possible medical intervention that might be needed.

One minute! I said to myself. *Here we go.*

A shout over the intercom: "Thirty seconds!" By this time we had eyes on the objective. I could see no threats on the outside, but I didn't expect to see anything either. My bird was the first to land, and I was the first to dismount with my Marine teammate next to me. I pushed forward about thirty yards and took a knee facing the objective. The team formed up together, and we moved toward the school.

I had cleared an entire school during my time in Iraq, so I felt like I knew what was to come. There would be long hallways, opposing doors, and open classrooms. In Iraq, my team breached what felt like a hundred doors, and we ran out of shotgun rounds by the time we were done. It was a learning experience that I assumed would come in handy on this mission.

My "experience" didn't help on this mission. What we encountered was totally different from what I anticipated. This abandoned school looked like a bomb had been dropped on it. There were two levels from what I could see, but the top level, at some point, had partially collapsed and had experienced excessive water damage that masked where the bottom floor started and the collapsed floor began.

Most military units—as well as those in other organizations like BORTAC—have a systematic approach to clearing a building. All SOPs are somewhat similar. I would typically clear the lowest level of any building first since it represents an immediate threat and it's the breach and entry point.

It is difficult to explain in detail how we swept through and cleared that wreck of a school. By the end of the mission, we had fine-tooth-combed every inch of the place and found only an area where Matt and Sweat may have shacked up for the night and heated up a quick meal.

It was frustrating. At times it felt like we were on their tail, and at others they seemed to be long gone. We tracked for several more days, looking for signs of where these two inmates might have been. We searched many abandoned structures, but by the end of the week, I felt like we might not catch these guys.

We were running long hours and days for almost a week before we were given a night off.

I was bummed because it was a Friday and my daughter's birthday was on Saturday and I was stuck in New York. I asked Chris Voss how he felt about me going home for the weekend to catch my daughter's birthday and then head back on a Monday. He was completely comfortable with that idea and got approval from SOS Larimore.

I bought my airline ticket and was ready to head home in the morning for the luau party I had so meticulously planned. I had been planning a luau party for my daughter Star, and I wanted to be there. I had spent so many years missing her birthday and I was excited I was actually going to make it for the celebration. Since we had the night off, we decided to grab a pizza and some beer at a local pub. To our surprise, it was karaoke night.

One of my teammates (I'll just call him "Bubba" for operational security reasons) was a monster of a man, our own version of Captain America, but he was more on the quiet side in public. He decided to sign himself up for a song, and so did Chris Voss. I am a massive fan of karaoke myself, but I wanted to see what my competition was like before I picked my song.

I couldn't believe my ears: Bubba chose "Ice Ice Baby." I was excited to hear what he had. I can't tell you it was terrible because all I remember is that when he took off his shirt, the crowd went wild. This is a legend that is almost certainly still circulating among BORTAC teams and maybe even in the town of Dannemora.

Voss picked "Plush," the classic Stone Temple Pilots song. This was perfect for him. His voice and confident posture made it even more awesome. And when I thought it couldn't get better, he would throw a random perfect-form head kick in the air. I was scared he would kill someone, but thankfully he didn't. Again, the crowd went wild.

I closed out the night with a little Cyndi Lauper: "Time After Time." I wasn't terrible, but it certainly wasn't memorable. By the end of the night our amateurish singing helped us blow off a lot of steam, something that we needed to do after almost a week of chasing false intelligence and conducting fruitless searches.

Sometimes it is better to hear different sides of the same story to get into the details of what happened and see it from another point of view. This is how Bubba remembered that night, and I think it describes the entire "karaoke experience" far better than I can. I think Bubba may have been more into it. In Bubba's own words:

The manhunt had seemingly gone cold after a week without any evidence to verify that David Sweat and Richard Matt were still in the area. The decision was made to recall BORTAC back to El Paso on a Monday. We had a few days to gather our equipment and prep everything for the flight back, but after having done some local intel gathering, I discovered that there was karaoke that night at a local watering hole called Olive Ridley's.

I make it a point to test out my rendition of "Ice Ice Baby" in every town I visit, so I was eager to check Plattsburgh off my list. It didn't take much convincing since there wasn't much else to do on a Wednesday night, especially in Plattsburgh, New York, so when 2100 rolled around, the entire team loaded up in our van and headed for the bar.

We arrived just as the DJ was beginning to open up the mic, and a few of us threw our names in immediately. I put in my usual selections: "Ice Ice Baby" by Vanilla Ice, "Boulevard of Broken Dreams" by Green Day, and "Inside Out" by Eve 6. Vargas put in to sing some Cyndi Lauper, and Voss went with his tried and true "Plush" by the Stone Temple Pilots.

When the DJ called me up, I waited in anticipation as the opening beat to "Ice Ice Baby" began to play. Most people immediately recognized what song was being played, and I got the feeling that they believed it would either be good or completely wretched. Luckily I knew every line of the song, and the screen with the lyrics was just there as a formality.

I began the rap, hitting every line and moving about the stage to the extent that the corded mic would allow. The crowd was loving it, and so was the DJ, chiming in every now and then with some of the chorus lyrics. When I was done, I got the usual hoots and hollers, which I've come to expect because I know that's the one song I can sing where I own the stage. Afterward, the DJ said that was the best rendition of "Ice Ice Baby" he had ever heard. He gave me a high five for my performance, and I made my way back to the table with the other guys to experience their praise.

Next up from our group was Voss. He's a child of the grunge age from when he was in Ranger Battalion up in Fort Lewis, just outside of Tacoma, Washington. Like me, he owned the song, and you could tell from his body language that he was totally into it. While he sang, Cavazos, who typically goes from sober to drunk in about four beers, started shouting: "Do a kick!" referring to Voss's background in tae kwon do. Since there was no reason not to, Voss obliged and threw a kick every now and then.

Soon after Voss finished, Vargas made his way up to the stage to belt out some Cyndi Lauper. I can only imagine what was going through the minds of some of the other patrons at the bar when they saw a six-foot-tall, stocky Mexican dude getting up there to sing "Time After Time." He did, and did an excellent job, much to my surprise.

When it was my turn again, I sang "Boulevard of Broken Dreams." For this song I have a freestyle version that I keep in my back pocket for when I start to get tipsy. Much like "Ice Ice Baby," I had rehearsed it countless times in the past, and I managed to go off the lyrics and turn it into my own rap. The DJ, again, thought that was impressive, and I was beginning to feel that we had established a good rapport with him.

When I made it back to our table, Vargas put his hand on my shoulder and said: "What do you think about the next time you go up, you take your shirt off for the crowd, and I'll come in and tell you to put it back on? That way we don't get kicked out."

It took me a fraction of a second to laugh and say: "Fuck yeah! Let's do it!" "Hell yeah," he said. "While you are putting your shirt back on, I'll take the mic and fill in for you." At 0030, and after all of us had a lot to drink, that sounded like a great idea. We're a bunch of alpha males at a bar, and in our minds, there's no one to tell us no.

When the rotation came around again and the DJ called my name, I walked up to the stage knowing full well what I was about to do, and Vargas was right at the edge, ready to jump in to play his role. As "Inside Out" started to play, I began singing along as I had a handful of times before.

Just before the instrumental break in the middle of the song, I looked briefly at Vargas to let him know I was about to do it and got the confirmation from his shit-eating grin. As soon as the instrumental hit, my shirt came off—inside out, ironically enough—to complement the song. Vargas rushed in and scolded me as planned and told me to put my shirt back on.

I could hear some hoots coming from the audience as I stood there partially inebriated and totally shirtless. I handed Vargas the mic as he filled in for me as the song played. I started putting my shirt back on, but because it had been inside out, one of the sleeves got caught up somewhere else inside the shirt and made it difficult to slip back on.

I only realized this after I had pulled it over my head and was trying to force my head and left arm through the openings that were all twisted up. I was standing there struggling with my shirt only covering my head and arms and I felt like I was trying to piece together a jigsaw puzzle. I eventually had to take it off again and fix the problem. When I got my shirt back on, I took the mic back from Vargas and finished off what was left of the song like nothing had happened.

The guys at the table looked like they were pissing themselves with laughter from watching me struggle, but I couldn't help but laugh with them too. That was the end of my song selection, even though others were still singing. We left Olive Ridley's at about 0130 and headed back to our hotel to call it a night.

We received a call early Saturday morning about a possible sighting of Matt and Sweat in a nearby marsh. Because the Black Hawk was in for maintenance, two A-Star helicopters (Airbus AS350) were provided to the BORTAC team with the doors removed and we responded to the call. As we approached the location, there was no viable landing zone (LZ), so local units on the ground halted traffic, and we landed in the middle of the highway.

We bolted out of the helos (slang for "helicopters") and began our patrol at the point of the last sighting, which was right off the highway. After a lengthy patrol and local units talking to residents of the area, it was discovered that the sighting was false and that two girls had been playing in the marsh but were mistaken for the escapees. This was common, as we had responded to multiple calls of supposed sightings. We loaded up on the helos and returned to base.

Once back at base, we recovered for a few hours, but then another call came in of shots being fired at a passing RV on one of the local roads. Again we scrambled, boarded the birds, and responded to the call. The A-Star is a fairly small bird, not built for a large transport capacity, so Voss and I boarded the one helo and the rest of the team made their way there by vehicle.

When we arrived, there was no viable LZ, so the decision was made to land on the highway again, just down the road from the site of the incident. We jumped off the helo and, as if it had been coordinated, two patrol cars drove up, one of which was driven by Major Guess, the incident commander. We jumped on the hoods of the vehicles, and they drove us to the scene. As we arrived, we saw the road lined with law enforcement spread every twenty-five yards, staring into the wood line.

At the site of the incident, we were shown to a residence within the vicinity of what had been reported. The people who lived there had reported that the trailer next to their home had been broken into and that grape-flavored liquor had been spilled and stolen from there. We conducted a search of the area, but could not find any good sign to follow.

It was at this time that FBI HRT (Hostage Rescue Team) was moving toward our location from about three-quarters of a mile away. We pushed over to a nearby trail near the marsh that was right next to the residence and held a line for HRT to meet up with us. HRT pushed until they came to the marsh on the opposite side of us.

Seeing that there was no sign of the escapees on their end, they decided to halt their patrol. We broke down our line and reconvened on the highway to discuss the next course of action. After having been on scene for over an hour with no activity, there was talk about returning to the TOC, but everyone felt unsure about that because of the nature of the call.

As Voss was walking back to us along the highway, one of the state patrolmen approached him and told him that one of his men had heard what he believed to be coughing coming from the woods. There were no other patrols out at that time in the area, so we formed up into a patrol formation and entered the wood line to investigate.

Walking in a wedge formation, we made our way along a path up to the trailer that had been broken into and met with some of the BORTACers from the Swanton SOD. They joined our patrol, and we headed down an embankment to push further. We moved approximately one hundred yards into the forest when we decided that a cough could not have been heard from so far back.

Not having seen any sign, we turned around and headed directly back to the highway. This was a slight variation from the path we patrolled coming in. Once we neared the highway, the brush became thick, and we were forced into a Ranger file where we had to negotiate a small embankment next to the marsh.

Cavazos was point, followed by Marinalarena, me, and Voss. The other patrol members were held back by the terrain. As the four of us made it up the hill, we naturally split into a staggered formation. I was now just behind Cavazos when I heard him say: "Police! Let me see your hands."

Even though I was right behind him, I could not see what he was looking at, but I pointed my weapon in that direction mirroring his posture. I knew that he had to have seen something for him to break the silence and present his weapon. As I held with Cavazos, Voss pushed around to the right to get a better angle on what Cavazos had seen.

Out of my peripheral vision, I saw Voss point his weapon and start giving commands. In that moment, the loudest noise I heard was Voss's safety being switched off on his weapon. The subject, from Voss's account, raised his head and briefly stared at Voss. Then in an instant, he started fumbling with a shotgun he held in an attempt to aim it at Voss. Voss recognized this and began firing.

I cannot recall accurately how many rounds were fired, even in the moments after the incident. It was all over in about three seconds. When the shooting ceased, we formed a 360 around the area, and I moved directly to the subject with Cavazos. There I saw a body with a shotgun near his hands. I pushed to the other side of it to provide cover for Cavazos, who moved the shotgun away from the subject's hands. I could tell though, by the disfiguration throughout the man's head, that he was deader than shit.

To be honest, I did not fear anything until immediately after the shooting. The announcement of shots fired and "One down hard" was made over the radio, and I could see troopers running above us near the highway. The shooting took place just below the hill leading up to the highway, so the troopers were on the scene relatively quickly, running with weapons at the low ready.

I just feared that in the anxiety of the situation we would have a blue-on-blue incident. Fortunately, those fears soon subsided as the troopers got down to our location and gained situational awareness. One problem remained: Who the fuck did we just shoot? It could have been a hunter, a bounty hunter, a vigilante, or just some idiot who pointed a gun at the cops and paid for it.

Truth is, at that time we didn't have a clue as to who this was, as his face was badly devastated by the rounds. Using the biometrics we had been briefed on, one of the troopers inspected the back of the downed subject and verified that it was Richard Matt by the "Mexico Forever" tattoo on his back.

A huge feeling of relief and excitement enveloped everyone there. But once that faded, we knew we needed to refocus to the mission at hand, because David Sweat was still on the loose. We began securing the perimeter so that the investigators could conduct their work, but ultimately we found no signs of David Sweat. We returned to base that evening.

Back at the TOC, we were interviewed by the investigators and had our pictures taken for their records. Counseling was offered to us in case we were at all traumatized by the event, but none of us felt the need for it. I for one, when I got back to my hotel room, took a shower and had a drink as I watched the news reports come out describing what had happened that day. We still had to be at work the next day, all except for Voss, who had to take administrative leave required by Border Patrol policy. I went to bed and slept comfortably, and I imagine that all my teammates did the same thing.

I flew home Saturday to enjoy my daughter's birthday. I watched the news and started to set up the bounce castle when I saw on the report that Richard Matt was killed by U.S. Border Patrol agents. I looked over at my father and asked him to turn the volume up. I couldn't believe what I was hearing. My team was scheduled to come back a few days after me, but they were called in because of some new intelligence. They had walked in on Matt's final position, and one of the members of my team was able to engage the threat as Matt elevated his shotgun on him.

My father asked if I was okay. As tears trickled down my face, I had to explain to him that I was on that mission the night before and had come home for the party. To add salt to my wounds, I was not only the team medic, but I had been trained in a new program for SOG as a Crisis Response member. In the event that there was an incident in SOG, they would contact me or one of the other trained members for support.

Within minutes of watching the news, I received a call from a familiar number that I wasn't ready for. I am not at liberty to disclose the contents of the call. But I can say that it left me in tears that I wasn't there with the team. Chris Voss was the person who had made the engagement, and I was hurt that I couldn't be there for him.

This was the first time in my career that I had chosen my family over work. I was extremely conflicted. I chose to be with my daughter for her birthday and not with my team for the mission. I left them without a designated BORSTAR medic, and I was at my daughter's party with my heart torn by whether or not it was the right decision.

After the party was over and the friends and family left, I was left alone with my thoughts. I have lived a life dedicated to serving a greater purpose. I believed in the mission and the men even though I knew how much my kids have missed during my life when I was away on missions and how much I had missed in theirs. The mission and my path had started to blur.

The whole ordeal had left me confused. The last thing my team deserved was a half-invested medic. My priorities had changed, and I decided it was best to resign and shift gears in life. It was time to put this chapter behind me and start a new career.

11

BORDER SECURITY AND IMMIGRATION POLICY

I don't think it's a secret that our current immigration system can be improved. In writing this book, my goal has been to establish what the day-to-day operations of a Border Patrol agent entail. I felt that I could achieve that goal by breaking down my own personal accounts.

Immigration is one of the most talked about topics of our time. Presidential candidates use the term "immigration reform" to persuade voters, which has proven successful, but if we dissect immigration policy as a whole, we see few significant changes in the past fifty-plus years.

This is not a Democratic or Republican issue as much as it's a human issue that needs to be addressed. In the military, I was always told that if I bring up an issue, I must have a solution.

In 2009 there was a significant overhaul attempt from a non-partisan group called the "Gang of Eight." Four Democrats and four Republicans came together to try and fix a broken system. They proposed an extensive immigration reform bill to satisfy both political parties and provide the answers to several issues. I am still not clear as to why this didn't pass. But it was the most comprehensive attempt of our time.

One of the most prominent challenges facing our country is the inability to separate border security from immigration policy. Independently, both border security and immigration policy are important, and we should have an informed discussion and find ways to improve both. It seems that every time a news story shows large groups of people entering the United States illegally, the dialogue shifts quickly from "those poor migrants" to "our border is wide open to terrorists." Seemingly, each side of the argument is oblivious to the other's position. We can debate both sides of this dialogue, and we should. But until there is a fundamental understanding that border security is not immigration policy, and vice versa, we will change neither for the better.

The most fundamental question we must ask is: What does a "secure border" really mean? It is ironic that if you ask people if they want a secure border, most will say yes. However, if you ask them to describe a secure border, their answers are vastly different. Security in general is one of those concepts that people practice (whether they notice or not) every day: locking a car door when shopping, strapping a purse over the head, or keeping dollar bills in the front pocket.

In my estimation, a secure border is a dynamic and relative state predicated on risk. We all assess risk throughout our lives. We have people and assets we want to protect, and, based on our assessment, we mitigate risk to do so. For example, most people feel secure in their homes. They may live in a gated community, have bolt locks on exterior doors, or have a monitored alarm system or other means of feeling secure. Conversely, others choose not to take many—or any—of these measures. Why? The reason is clear. It is because each person takes what they believe to be reasonable action to minimize risk in their lives, but they also know that no matter how much protection they might have in their home, they cannot guarantee that their homes will never be broken into.

Why should our border be any different? People's perception of a secure border may mean Border Patrol agents patrolling the line; they may see integrated surveillance towers and an eighteen-foot border wall, hear the helicopters in the night sky, and "feel secure." However, does deploying personnel, technology, and infrastructure equate to a secure border? It's a good start, but unless risk is taken into account, it provides merely an illusion of security. For example, for many years, the San Diego Sector was held up as the "model" for border security. With sixty linear miles of border, the sector has most of its area of operations under surveillance. They boast the highest percentage of fenced or walled border in the country, which thousands of agents patrol. People from other states will point to San Diego and ask: "Why can't our border be secure like theirs?" Those same people will be surprised to know that 85 percent of all sophisticated drug tunnels found along the U.S. border were dug in the San Diego Sector. Is that a secure border?

Border security can ultimately be achieved if one recognizes it as a dynamic condition based on evolving risks and not as an end state. A good place to start is to define what a secure border looks (and doesn't look) like and then strive to do better. If you can't define the problem, no solution will work.

There is no "point solution" to border security, and I won't attempt to offer one. What I will do, based on my experience as a Border Patrol agent, as well as on my tight connection with current agents, is suggest some commonsense actions that can help lead to a more secure border. As with any problem or situation requiring a resolution, people will often turn to the obvious questions of "How do we fix it?" or "What does winning look like?" However, you must first consider whether the problem you are trying to solve has an obvious solution or, if not, what the trade-offs are in such a situation. Often, the solution lies in doing your best to maintain and stabilize a certain level of acceptable chaos rather than trying to completely solve the problem.

To illustrate this point, consider a forest fire. A forest fire is an unwanted event taking place in a habitat that is destroyed by its presence. A small fire can inflict significant damage, while a large-scale fire is often catastrophic. Therefore, you must consider significantly different factors when approaching how to prevent and fight forest fires. The goal is to always put out the fire completely and do everything possible to prevent a new one from sparking. It is this zero-sum approach that is often used when viewing border security and attempting to illustrate what winning looks like and what the desired end state should be.

Despite the lofty optimism of many pseudo border experts, this is a completely unrealistic approach. Securing the border is more akin to preserving a wildland habitat rather than extinguishing a forest fire. Border security must be viewed through the lens of maintenance, attention, acceptable risk and loss, and the understanding that the goal is harmony between two diametrically opposing concepts: security and freedom.

Border security by its very nature is predicated on the restriction of movement between two places. The minute a border goes up, an instant amount of friction and conflict is created, no matter how friendly the opposing parties may be with one another.

Therefore, the level of security must be balanced against the level of freedom. The dial must not be turned too far in either direction. Too much security results in a completely locked-down border with no humanitarian considerations and limited trade due to extensive security precautions and the inefficiency of screening processes. Conversely, too much freedom promotes a chaotic and totally lawless and unregulated border, where corruption and crime are essentially unrestricted.

In practical terms, consider the current border security models from around the world and their corresponding impacts on the populations of their nation and their neighbors. On the one hand, you have an essentially unrestricted border between countries like Pakistan and Afghanistan. These are lawless border areas, ruled by conflicting tribes, where smugglers and various forms of traffickers operate with no fear of disruption by either government. A similar assessment can be made of the border shared by Somalia, Kenya, and Ethiopia, an area where members of Al-Shabaab are able to operate with relative impunity.

Although it may sound counterintuitive, this is the result when the freedom dial is pushed to its limit. Freedom is not merely a modern construct of the American economic system, nor is it limited to the pursuit of happiness as defined by Western and first-world ideals. Freedom has an ugly and violent side in most of the world. For some, it is the freedom to do whatever you want and be limited only by your own morality. Freedom allows more powerful groups and their members to exert their will on and dominate others, using their power to further their status. It is only our modern version of freedom that exists within the confines of Western rule of law and our cosmopolitan norms, and this version of freedom is curtailed by restrictions imposed by laws and a certain level of security.

At the other end of the dial is a security state where the government has a monopoly on violence and the security and survival of the state is at the forefront. Enough historical examples exist—such as the Berlin Wall that defined East and West Germany throughout the Cold War, or the modern border between North Korea and South Korea—to illustrate what happens when there is a nearly impervious and impenetrable border. When the security dial is turned to its limit, the results are just as devastating and repressive as the complete lack of security. To be both effective and humane, border security cannot be wielded like a sledgehammer to immediately resolve a conflict or eliminate an enemy. It must be carefully and deliberately curated like a chemical compound and subsequently monitored to ensure stability.

The questions then become: What sort of border do we as Americans wish to have? What adequately represents our values and morals, and what sort of border can we envision? How do we have a border where trade and humanitarian considerations simultaneously exist alongside a security posture focused on protecting our nation, as well as degrading criminal organizations operating on both sides of the border? The dial should be set somewhere in the middle, and there should also be enough flexibility to regularly adjust it in one direction or another. These minor adjustments should be guided by both security concerns and humanitarian considerations to ensure that while remaining the land of freedom and opportunity, the United States should never compromise its own security and freedom.

Our border is not broken. It is misunderstood and neglected. When news anchors, so-called experts, and politicians commonly call CBP Customs and Border Patrol instead of its proper name, Customs and Border Protection, or erroneously juxtapose a Border Patrol agent with an ICE deportation officer, it is no wonder that our immigration system and border security does not get the attention it deserves.

The first step to finding a solution is to inform an attentive public that considers border security a national issue rather than a regional issue. The American people need to understand that border security is something they are entitled to even if they do not live along the southwest border. There needs to be a concerted effort between government officials, politicians, and actual border security professionals to educate the public on the reality of the current immigration system and border security process and create a way forward. Our borders require the same attention that was devoted to combating and preventing another terrorist attack after September 11, 2001.

The second step is to empower the men and women of the

U.S. Border Patrol to do their jobs efficiently and effectively. "Just hire more agents" is not the solution if you are looking to establish and maintain a professional and highly skilled workforce.

What the Border Patrol needs is highly skilled and highly trained personnel who are equipped with the latest technology to ensure that they can monitor, detect, deter, and respond. Although the current iteration of the Border Patrol Academy continues to improve its training and standards, the federal government has been slow to implement the latest technology along our southern border.

We have also been slow to implement a true "whole of government approach" when it comes to sending support personnel to assist with housing, feeding, and screening migrants and allowing the law enforcement personnel of the Border Patrol to remain in the field. Additional external assistance with nonessential law enforcement tasks can serve as a vital pressure relief valve for the frontline personnel of the Border Patrol. Although the new Border Patrol Processing Coordinator positions are a step in the right direction, much more can and should be done.

The Border Patrol needs to finally and decisively address its continuous retention and recruiting shortfalls and maximize its current personnel. The Border Patrol needs to get back to its core mission and focus more on agents on the ground and less on headquarters and sector functions. Permanent headquarters and sector assignments should be limited to a select group of high-ranking leadership roles. All other assignments should be on a rotational basis and limited to only a few years. To increase recruitment and retention it is also vital that the Border Patrol implement some sort of mobility system to allow for greater relocation opportunity.

A possible solution would be to implement a tier structure for locations, similar to what exists in the U.S. Secret Service and the FBI. A newly hired agent would be stationed at a Tier 3 location along the southern border for a minimum term of three to five years. After the completion of this rotation, the agent may elect to stay at the Tier 3 location for another predetermined term that could be tied to a monetary retention bonus, or they could place their name into a selection pool for a Tier 2 or Tier 1 location.

The same process would apply to agents at a mid-career point where they would once again be given the option to relocate or remain at their current duty station. Although the mechanisms and policies surrounding such a program would have to be worked out, the concept is predicated on the realistic understanding that the initial locations and the subsequent lack of options is what restricts many from applying to and staying with the Border Patrol.

Regardless of how you feel about any or all of these policy prescriptions, it is undeniable that a problem that is ignored will remain unsolved. The men and women of the Border Patrol deserve not only our respect but also our attention and consideration. We must take an interest in our nation's border and the men and women who dedicate their lives to protecting it.

12

BORDER VIOLENCE AND SHOOTINGS

One of the most misguided and dangerous claims about the U.S. Border Patrol is that the use of lethal force is not only routine but is so common that it is essentially a standard way of doing business. Many reasonable, well-intentioned, and otherwise well-informed and educated people believe that migrants, illegal aliens, drug mules, and human smugglers are regularly shot and killed along the Mexican border by unrestrained Border Patrol agents who are granted complete freedom to dispense lethal violence without hesitation.

This is false and completely exaggerated. Most of the violence we hear about on the border happens on the Mexican side. The cartels constantly have to manage their pipeline of drugs. At the same time, other drug trafficking organizations are trying to gain ground on new territories while maintaining order in their own ranks. This leads to turf wars. Understandably, turf wars are the source of the majority of danger on the border.

If these conflicts crossed over to the American side, there

would be extreme consequences for the individuals who didn't restrict this violence to the southern side of the border. To elaborate, as it stands, the Border Patrol apprehends drugs often, but as drugs are pushed north at one point of the border, double or triple the amount is potentially smuggled elsewhere.

Misinformation is our greatest threat. There is a diverse group of people who provide bogus information regarding the situation on our southern border. Some are politically motivated and habitually lie and mislead the public about their own parties' goals and ambitions. Others weaponize these misguided claims to sell clicks and generate ad revenue. In contrast, many others engage in a perverse outrage economy, hoping to push a social and political agenda among their constituents.

Of course, many of these people are guided by perverse incentives and are not interested in reporting facts or having an honest discussion about specific incidents or general policies and practices within the agency. Many who publicly demand reform and change refuse to make contact with the most basic facts. They refuse to acknowledge successes and restraint where they obviously exist, and they demand penalties for the most reasonable and understandable uses of force.

As I have previously tried to counter common misconceptions and outright lies about our immigration system, it is crucial to do the same thing to further the discussion on the use of force in the Border Patrol.

It is important to talk about the numbers in order to make an informed discussion. But before I present relevant statistics, I want to first allow you to make your own predictions about this topic. This allows you to test your intuition against the facts and potentially demonstrate what partisan hyperbole and politically motivated chatter does to obscure reality.

To be as inclusive as possible, we will include all incidents where an agent used their firearm in the field, not just those where there was a loss of life. To bound the problem, let's examine the period between fiscal year 2019 and fiscal year 2022. How many Border Patrol agents do you think used their weapons during those four years? What number do you think is reasonable, and what number are you thinking? Is it fifteen hundred? Is it a thousand? Are you thinking that maybe a few hundred shootings took place in those four years? The real number is forty. Only forty shootings took place along the border between FY 2019 and FY 2022, while millions of people were apprehended and processed.

Now let's do the same thought experiment on how many agents were assaulted during this same four-year period. What number comes to mind? How many agents were attacked and assaulted by people crossing illegally? Do you think it was five hundred? Maybe close to a thousand? Perhaps as many as fifteen hundred? The actual number of agent assaults is just over twenty-one hundred. There were over twenty-one hundred separate incidents where agents were attacked, hit with rocks, stabbed, cut, or otherwise injured. Given the simple game theory and probability comparison, an agent is over fifty times more likely to be assaulted than they are to use lethal force to defend themselves from such an attack.

Why is this important? Why are we talking about the Border Patrol and how its agents use lethal force? It is important because we want to demonstrate that a highly trained and well-disciplined law enforcement organization should be the model for other agencies to follow, and it can be achieved through good training.

The reason it is also critical to highlight this characteristic about the Border Patrol is because unlike most police departments around the country, the Border Patrol operates in fairly isolated environments. Border Patrol agents are often alone when they encounter large groups of people attempting to cross the border to escape danger in their home country, but they also can have solo encounters with drug mules and traffickers who are far more dangerous when encountered in such scenarios.

And despite what is often reported in the media, one of the main orientations of the Border Patrol as an agency is humanitarianism and the preservation of life, not violence and force. In fact, this is where the virtues of strength, power, and restraint come from. These become virtues by knowing when to use them: when to inflict harm, and when not to, even when doing so may be the safer route to take.

In other parts of the world, strength and power can be misused at the expense of restraint. Police in totalitarian states can be violent toward peaceful protesters, or even toward those exercising civil disobedience, in an effort to demonstrate that further dissent will not be tolerated. Thankfully, we live in a society where we hold our law enforcement organizations to a higher standard. In fact, the freedom to scrutinize law enforcement agencies is a direct result of this exact model.

If we lived in a totalitarian and fascist society, as many dissenters and critics believe we do, we would not be scrutinizing and holding our law enforcement officials accountable. There would be no public outcry, there would be no protests, and there would be no calls for reform, because in a closed society ruled by an authoritative dictatorship, these very expressions of discontent would never be allowed.

This is the real paradox of power on display every day along our borders. Agents having the ability to exert their will through force, while having the restraint to not do so, even when not doing so preemptively may put their own lives in danger.

The career field has its dangers and challenges, but I firmly believe the biggest threat to the Border Patrol is the misinformation being spread through mainstream media and the lack of counter and correct information to take its place.

13

THE BORDER PATROL HISTORY AND LEGACY

During the course of this book, I have told you a great deal about the U.S. Border Patrol and how it evolved during my years of service. I have also mentioned that the Border Patrol was first formed in 1924 and thus is approaching its one hundredth anniversary of defending our nation. Now I want to tell you a bit more about this agency's history.

My fellow agents and I are part of that thin green line, that borderline, where battles are fought daily between the opposing extremes of life and death, justice and villainy, peace and chaos.

Those of us who have worn the gold badge and green uniform of the Border Patrol are part of a family with a rich and distinguished history steeped in tradition and honor. That family was not born from a bloodline but was bonded in life by a green one. The badge we wore has been given to only the few who earned the right to wear it. It represents all the Border Patrol agents who have come before me, served with me, serve today, and will serve tomorrow.

Each of us, from the agent patrolling the border to the one rescuing a child in distress, apprehending a criminal, serving on the joint terrorism task force or another special unit, or commanding the entire organization, has started out at the Border Patrol Academy as a trainee. We all graduated from what is considered one of the most difficult law enforcement academies in the country. This bond unites us, and those of us who have worn the badge and uniform of Border Patrol agent have a proud legacy of history, tradition, and esprit de corps.

The Border Patrol has been called upon countless times to render aid and assistance to our country, sometimes with little notice and at great risk, but the Border Patrol has always answered its nation's call for help. For generations, Border Patrol agents have charged into situations from which others would run to enforce the rule of law, save lives, assist our fellow men and women (whether illegal immigrants or citizens), or support and defend the Constitution in times of crisis or emergency.

Although the language in the statutes governing our work may have changed over the years, the primary mission of the Border Patrol is and has been to enforce the laws that protect America's homeland by the detection, interdiction, and apprehension of those who attempt to illegally enter or smuggle any person or contraband across our nation's sovereign borders. But this is not the only mission the Border Patrol has been tasked with over the course of its history. The following timeline provides some of the little-known historical facts and nontraditional missions of the U.S. Border Patrol.

The information below was provided to me by Joe Banco, author of *Honor First: The Story of the United States Border Patrol.*

1920s

The U.S Border Patrol had a humble beginning on May 28, 1924, with 450 patrol inspectors, many of whom were recruited from organizations such as the Texas Rangers; others included local sheriffs and deputies, cowboys and ranch hands, and appointees from the Civil Service Register. They began duty at the height of Prohibition, fighting rumrunners and engaging in border gunfights on a regular basis against determined smugglers who were skilled marksmen and horsemen themselves. Many perished in the line of duty.

1924–1933: Increased violence associated with liquor smuggling during the enactment of the Eighteenth Amendment, the Volstead Act (Prohibition), led to 238 officially recorded gunfights involving patrol inspectors in the El Paso, Texas, area alone.

Twenty-three patrol inspectors were killed in the line of duty.

The first African American Border patrol inspector was Paul L. D. Calloway, who entered duty in June 1924 at Niagara Falls. This was twenty-four years before the military began to be integrated.

1930s

On December 3, 1934, the first formal Border Patrol Training School was established at Camp Chigas in El Paso, Texas. The U.S. Border Patrol Academy would become known as the toughest law enforcement training school in the country, and was also one of the first to include training in the use of "modern" equipment and techniques such as radios, fingerprints, and telegraph, and which also included an intensive Spanish course.

The Border Patrol Mobile First Aid Units were formed in the late 1930s and were recognized by the American Red Cross for their response on September 20, 1938, to a head-on collision of two passenger trains near Tortuga, California, resulting in 11 dead and 139 injured. The Border Patrol inspectors of the Mobile First Aid Unit assisted in rescuing the injured, providing first aid, supplementing in recovery efforts, and protecting the scene from looters and souvenir hunters.

1940s

During World War II, the U.S. Border Patrol was placed in charge of Axis enemy alien detention camps at Fort Stanton, New Mexico; Fort Missoula, Montana; Fort Lincoln, North Dakota; Tuna Canyon, California; Tule Lake, California; Sharp Park, California; Santa Fe, New Mexico; Camp Algiers, Louisiana; Seagoville, Texas; Kennedy, Texas; and Crystal City, Texas.

Border Patrol inspectors were also responsible for

guarding/securing Axis enemy diplomats (Japanese, Germans, Italians, French Vichy) and their families at the Greenbrier Hotel at White Sulphur Springs, West Virginia; the Homestead Hotel at Hot Springs, Virginia; the Bedford Springs Hotel in Bedford, Pennsylvania; the Hershey Hotel in Hershey, Pennsylvania; and the Grove Park Inn in Asheville, North Carolina.

Per the request of the Department of State, Border Patrol inspectors traveled to Central and South America aboard Army transport ships to detain and escort those determined to be "dangerous enemy aliens" by the respective foreign nations. This was considered a measure of national defense and hemispheric security. Many of the detained enemy aliens would be repatriated to their native countries in exchange for American civilians being held in the Axis nations.

1950s

In 1951, the German federal government formally approved the creation of the Bundesgrenzschutz (Federal Border Guard), developed with help of U.S. Border Patrol inspectors assigned in the U.S. Army of Occupation.

In 1955, the U.S. Border Patrol became the original "Con Air," with Border Patrol pilots and aircraft transporting federal prisoners, including famous racketeers/gangsters such as Carlos Marcello and Mickey Cohen, for the Bureau of Prisons.

In 1956, Border Patrol inspectors helped process

I was selected to be the cadre for the Del Rio BORSTAR pre-selection. This was a water training day at Lake Amistad in Del Rio, Texas.

In this photo I was on detail at McAllen Sector with Del Rio Special Operations Detachment (SOD). I was the medic attached to BORTAC, activated in an effort to support a Border Patrol sector that was in need of manpower due to an influx of traffic.

Eagle Pass, Texas. This was a photo being sent around the sector of a little girl that looked no older than ten handing a note to a kneeling Border Patrol agent in the early morning fog.

SOG BORTAC training mission with other three-letter agencies. I was the BORSTAR agent attached.

Prepping for issuing a warrant in the Del Rio Sector SOD.

Found in a ranch in Eagle Pass, Texas. An illegal immigrant that was separated from her group in the middle of the summer wrote HELP with sticks she'd found in the area before she passed away due to extreme dehydration.

SOG BORTAC with a BORSTAR medic attached (me). On a UH-60 Blackhawk on our way to a mission to capture escaped convicts Matt and Sweat.

Del Rio BORTAC team (DIRTYBIRDS) with BORSTAR medic attached during a detail to McAllen Sector. In 2011–14 the McAllen Sector was the one of the busiest sectors for the Border Patrol in illegal immigration and drug smuggling.

BORSTAR new guy selfie. In the summer months it wasn't uncommon to search a group in our green shirts and some kind of rack system that carries ammo, water, medical supplies, and GPS.

This photo shows a search of two individuals stopped under suspicion of smuggling drugs illegally through the Eagle Pass area of operations.

Me during a detail to McAllen Sector.

Chris Smilo and me after graduating from BORSTAR
Class 22 Selection.

New guy photo in the Eagle Pass area of operations. If you
look in the rear of the photo you can see a small example of
the cane that we had to work with.

I was off duty in a government vehicle and witnessed another vehicle stopped in the middle of a freeway. I pulled up behind it and turned the lights on to maintain safety from a potentially hazardous situation. Once the proper authorities arrived, they arrested a drug smuggler that fell asleep at the wheel after a long night of transporting drugs.

In the front of a class formation at the FLETC Border Patrol Academy graduation. Class 880.

In formation during Border Patrol graduation in Artesia, New Mexico.

This is a graduation photo with my mother. Credentials and graduation certificate in hand.

Graduation photo with my classmate Nick Soto. We were both stationed in Eagle Pass North and had worked on the same unit.

BORSTAR cadre for Class 23 selection.

I was able to run a variant of the Army Combatives training to Eagle Pass, Texas, Border Patrol and teach several classes on hand-to-hand combat.

This was a selfie taken minutes before a mission to track down escaped convicts Matt and Sweat.

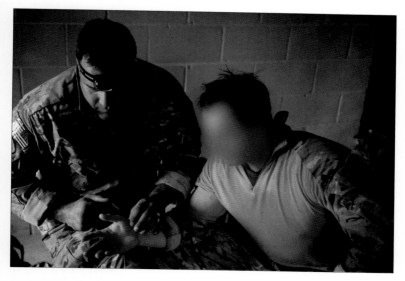

This BORTAC team member had a minor injury to his hand. I was doing a medical assessment and provided interventions to get him back into the fight for a training mission.

Chris Smilo and me practicing giving ourselves IVs after passing our EMT National Registry.

This is my full SOG team in 2015 during the infamous escaped convicts Matt and Sweat days.

This is a photo taken during BORSTAR Selection Class 22. Somewhere in this photo is me with my head deep in the mud regretting everything that had led me to this point. At the front of this photo is Alan Rogers.

Two BORTACers with me in the middle, waiting for the sun to go down to start a night operation.

A vehicle filled with bundles of marijuana that was stopped in the McAllen Sector.

Another loaded vehicle apprehension in the McAllen area of operations by Del Rio Special Operations Detachment.

A successful lay-up operation in McAllen area of operations that led to a load house filled with bundles of drugs.

Chris Smilo and me during swift water rescue training in the San Fernando Valley.

Class photo of the BORSTAR selection graduating Class 22 students and cadre members.

Absolutely ridiculous new guy photo in the Eagle Pass North area of operations.

BORSTAR training BORTAC in drown proofing techniques.

Hungarian refugees at Camp Kilmer, NJ, after the Hungarian Revolution against Communist rule.

1960s

On August 3, 1961, Border Patrolman (Associate Deputy Regional Commissioner) Leonard Gilman stopped one of the first reported airline hijacking attempts in the United States, subduing an armed hijacker after the plane landed in El Paso, Texas. Border Patrol inspectors and other law enforcement disabled the aircraft by shooting out the tires.

In August–October 1961, the U.S. Border Patrol assumed security for airline traffic to prevent hijackings, becoming the first sky marshals. President John F. Kennedy announced this to the nation, and twelve hours later, Border Patrol officers were riding and safeguarding commercial flights. The operation was coordinated by the Miami Sector, which assumed responsibility for the entire United States. The operation ended on October 23, 1961, with 355 USBP inspectors guarding 1,310 commercial flights.

In 1961, the Border Patrol was responsible for transporting attorney James Donovan to secret negotiations for the release of U-2 pilot Francis Gary Powers. In 1962, Border Patrol pilots transported Soviet spy Rudolf Ivanovich across the country and transferred him to a military aircraft to be flown to Berlin where he was exchanged for Powers. The story of the negotiations and exchange were made famous in the movie *Bridge of Spies*.

Border Patrol inspectors deployed in 1961 and 1962 to assist U.S. Marshals in protecting Martin Luther King, Jr., and the Freedom Riders and quelling racial disturbances in Montgomery and Selma, Alabama, as well as in Washington, DC.

The U.S. Border Patrol was instrumental in ending the "long night" of segregation in the American South and upholding civil rights and federal laws by deploying Border Patrol inspectors to Oxford, Mississippi, to protect James Meredith as he became the first African American student at the University of Mississippi on October 1, 1962. Of the 349 Border Patrol inspectors deployed, 72 were injured by rioters.

Border Patrol inspectors deployed to the University of Alabama in June 1963 to protect Vivian Malone and James Hood as they enrolled at the university in defiance of Governor George Wallace.

In December 1962, U.S. Border Patrol inspectors were directed by President Kennedy to assist in processing 1,113 Bay of Pigs prisoners being transferred from Cuba and in sending food and medical supplies to the Castro government in exchange for the prisoners. As part of the operation, several Patrol inspectors flew into Cuba with attorney James Donovan as he met with Fidel Castro for the final negotiations. The Patrol inspectors returned with the first group of Bay of Pigs freedom fighters.

In 1963, Border Patrol pilots and aircraft assisted in

evacuating Alcatraz Prison when it closed down, moving over two hundred convicts to other federal penitentiaries.

In October 1967, 120 Border Patrol inspectors were deployed to Washington, DC/Arlington, Virginia, to support the U.S. Marshals during the antiwar protest/riot at the Pentagon. The Patrol inspectors, deputized as U.S. Marshals, faced 50,000 protesters. A total of 682 demonstrators were arrested for disorderly conduct.

In April 1968, twenty-six Border Patrol inspectors, led by New Orleans Chief Patrol Inspector Charles Chamblee, deployed to provide additional security in Memphis, Tennessee, for marchers, including the King family, honoring Martin Luther King days after his assassination. The inspectors then deployed to Atlanta, Georgia, to assist in security for Dr. King's funeral services.

In May/June 1968, thirty-eight Patrol inspectors were deployed to Washington, DC, to assist U.S. Marshals and the National Park Service in maintaining good order in and around the Resurrection City encampment built on the National Mall and to ensure safety during the "Poor People's Marches."

January 1969, Border Patrol inspectors assisted the U.S. Secret Service and Capitol Police in providing security for the presidential inauguration. The U.S. Border Patrol continues to assist with security for every presidential inauguration to this day.

In September 1969, the Nixon administration initiated Operation Intercept/Cooperation to stem the flow of drugs at the border. Border Patrol agents deployed additional manpower to the southwest border and supplemented efforts between and at the Ports of Entry. This included providing air support and assisting in manning temporary air radar installations in remote areas of the border.

1970s

On February 27, 1973, President Nixon directed the deployment of fifty Border Patrol agents to assist U.S. Marshals during the seventy-one-day Native American uprising at Wounded Knee, South Dakota.

After the fall of South Vietnam on April 30, 1975, the U.S. began evacuating over 150,000 South Vietnamese and 50,000 Cambodians seeking freedom from communist regimes. The refugees were temporarily housed and processed at four military installations: Camp Pendleton, California; Eglin Air Force Base, Florida; Fort Chaffee, Arkansas; and Fort Indiantown Gap, Pennsylvania. Border Patrol agents were deployed to each of these locations to assist in processing the refugees for immigration/asylum.

On July 31, 1975, the first female Border Patrol agent, Christine Gee, graduated with the 107th session of the U.S. Border Patrol Academy. Gee and five other women graduated among the 223 trainees in the largest Border Patrol Academy class to date.

On July 17, 1978, Border Patrol agents apprehended

Kristina Berster, a member of the Baader-Meinhof Gang (Red Army Faction) terrorist organization. Berster and two associates were apprehended while illegally crossing the border from Canada into Vermont. Berster was wanted by the German government and Interpol as a suspect in a series of bombings, bank robberies, kidnappings, and hijackings.

1980s

In April 1980, Cuban Premier Fidel Castro forcibly deported 125,000 Cuban nationals, many of whom were political dissidents or criminals. Border Patrol agents provided security details, hospital security, and riot control at processing centers at Key West, Florida; Eglin Air Force Base, Florida; Fort Chaffee, Arkansas; Fort Indiantown Gap, Pennsylvania; and Oakdale, Louisiana.

Border Patrol agents have played a key role in protecting international athletes and providing security at both the Summer and Winter Olympic Games when they have been held in the United States, including at the 1980 Winter Olympics in Lake Placid, New York, and the 1984 Summer Olympics in Los Angeles, California.

In 1982, U.S. Border Patrol Agents were deployed to control an inmate uprising at the Krome Detention Center in Florida.

On May 6, 1984, the U.S. Border Patrol Tactical Unit (BORTAC) was established. BORTAC provides the Department of Justice, and now the Department of Homeland Security, with a specially equipped tactical unit for rapid response, direct action, and special reconnaissance deployments to law enforcement situations and intelligence-based threats requiring special weapons, tactics, techniques, and procedures in defense of our national security. BORTAC missions range from urban high-risk arrest/search warrants to rural interdictions in the vast, unpopulated border regions throughout the United States. BORTAC also performs foreign internal defense operations, training, and advising missions with foreign law enforcement and military for strategic global allies.

In 1987, BORTAC worked with the Drug Enforcement Administration to conduct counter-narcotics operations in South America during Operation Snowcap. BORTAC members participated in narcotic eradication efforts, including targeting clandestine drug laboratories and illicit airfields and interdicting illicit shipments of precursor chemicals and cocaine.

In 1987, U.S. Border Patrol Agents were deployed to control inmate uprisings at the Marana Detention Facility in Arizona, the Atlanta Federal Penitentiary in Georgia, and the Oakdale Detention Facility in Louisiana.

In October 1989, U.S. Border Patrol agents were deployed to provide security and humanitarian assistance after the magnitude 6.9 earthquake hit San Francisco.

On September 15, 1989, Border Patrol agents assigned to the Houlton Sector in Maine assisted the Edmundson Police and Royal Canadian Mounted Police in a cross-border weapons and terrorism investigation involving four members of a Colombian hit team arrested with machine guns, sniper rifles, pistols, and other weapons that they had smuggled across the border into Canada. The Colombian hit team was tasked with freeing the nephew of Pablo Escobar, who was in a Canadian jail for smuggling five hundred kilograms of cocaine into Canada.

1990s

1990/1991—U.S. Border Patrol Agents were deployed to various U.S. international airports on counterterrorism security detail in support of Operation Desert Storm.

In April 1992, 387 U.S. Border Patrol agents were deployed to provide security and quell civil disturbances after the Rodney King verdict in Los Angeles, California. Those deployed to the LA riots included members of the Horse Patrol, members of BORTAC, and six pilots and helicopters. Working with the Los Angeles Police Department, the Border Patrol agents made 140 arrests, including 20 felony arrests, and seized 123 weapons, including a live hand grenade.

In August/September 1992, Border Patrol agents were deployed to south Florida to provide humanitarian relief and law enforcement support efforts in the aftermath of Hurricane Andrew.

After the July 27, 1996, Centennial Olympic Park bombing, 354 students and 65 instructors from the Border Patrol Academy deployed within 48 hours to provide security for the 1996 Summer Olympics in Atlanta, Georgia.

In 1996, the United States and Canada formed the first Integrated Border Enforcement Team (IBET) to combat smuggling and illegal immigration on the northwest border between Blaine, Washington, and British Columbia. The primary IBET members consisted of the U.S. Border Patrol, U.S. Customs, and U.S. Coast Guard on the American side, and the Royal Canadian Mounted Police and Canadian Customs on the Canadian side.

The Border Patrol Search, Trauma, and Rescue Unit (BORSTAR) had its birth in El Paso, Texas, in 1987 as the first medical rescue team in the U.S. Border Patrol. The concept of a rescue unit of medically trained Border Patrol agents would expand to other sectors, including San Diego in 1998, and a national BORSTAR program would be established that same year.

In June 1998, the Border Safety Initiative was established to reduce injuries and prevent deaths of those crossing the southwest border illegally. The initiative's four elements included prevention through education/public service announcements and identification of dangerous crossing areas, search-and-rescue operations, identification of deceased border crossers, and tracking and recording.

In 1999, the U.S. Border Patrol became the largest

uniformed federal law enforcement agency in the nation with 8,351 Border Patrol agents.

On December 14, 1999, Border Patrol agents played a significant role in the arrest of Ahmed Ressam, "the Millennium Bomber." Ressam was detained by Customs officers at the Port Angeles, Washington, ferry terminal, and his vehicle was seized with bomb-making material in the trunk. Ressam broke free and tried to escape but was captured by another Customs officer. Border Patrol agents were contacted and apprehended him on immigration violations. Working with the U.S.-Canada Integrated Border Enforcement Team, the Border Patrol confirmed that he was a known terrorist. Ressam's capture foiled his plan to bomb the Los Angeles International Airport.

2000s

On November 25, 1999, five-year-old Cuban Elian Gonzalez landed in south Florida after he was found floating in an inner tube off the Ft. Lauderdale coast. Elian's mother perished on the journey from Cuba. An international custody battle ensued, and the Clinton administration decided to return Elian to his father in Cuba. On April 22, 2000, Elian was removed from Miami by the Border Patrol Tactical Unit (BORTAC) and reunited with his father as part of Operation Reunion.

Within forty-eight hours following the terrorist attacks on September 11, 2001, the U.S. Border Patrol deployed 318 agents to nine U.S. international airports (JFK, LaGuardia, Newark, Boston, San Francisco, Dallas, Houston, Detroit, and Seattle) for security as part of Operation Safe Passage.

Blaine Sector Border Patrol agents apprehended Lee Boyd Malvo in Bellingham, Washington, on December 19, 2001, and processed him and his mother for deportation to their native Jamaica. They were transported to the Seattle Immigration and Naturalization Service (INS) Deportation Center where they were reprocessed by other INS officers and released. At the time of apprehension, Malvo was with John Allen Muhammad. Muhammed and Malvo would later become known as the DC Snipers after going on a three-week shooting spree in October 2002, killing ten and wounding three in the greater Washington, DC, area (DC/VA/MD). Border Patrol information was used to confirm their identities.

In February 2002, the U.S. Border Patrol deployed 261 Border Patrol agents to help provide security for the 2002 Winter Olympics in Salt Lake City, Utah.

From August 28, 2004, to December 2004, eighteen Border Patrol agents led by BORTAC deployed to Jordan to begin training Iraqi Department of Border Enforcement (DBE) border police/guard members.

January 22, 2005, the first Border Support Team (BST), led by BORTAC members, deployed to Iraq. Thirteen Border Patrol agents and six CBP officers deployed after receiving training from BORTAC in El

Paso, Texas. The mission of BST is to provide advisory and training assistance at international border crossing locations in Iraq, as well as to assist the Iraqi DBE Customs, Immigration, and Border Police.

In September 2005, two hundred Border Patrol agents from across the country were deployed to New Orleans for Hurricane Katrina humanitarian and law enforcement relief efforts. These included Border Patrol pilots, canine teams, and BORTAC and BORSTAR personnel to provide tactical law enforcement support and search-and-rescue operations.

In 2006, Border Patrol agents began deploying to Afghanistan as part of CBP two-man teams supporting the Afghanistan Border Management Task Force (BMTF) in mentoring Afghan border control officials. The BMTF was a mixed civilian and military task force whose primary goal was to assist the Afghan government by providing subject matter expertise for oversight of capacity building and training relating to customs and border operations.

2010s

In 2010, Border Patrol agents became part of the "permanent" CBP presence in Afghanistan under the DHS attaché. Border Patrol agents made up the majority of the eleven authorized positions, and one was designated as the Afghanistan Border Management Task Force program director.

On July 22, 2012, while deployed in Herat, Afghanistan, Border Patrol Agent (Assistant Chief) Eric Gough responded to an Afghan National Police guard opening fire with an AK-47 on Border Management Task Force personnel, including contractors, and engaged and killed the shooter. Three BMTF members were killed and two severely injured during the attack. Assistant Chief Gough provided critical first aid to one of the injured, saving his life.

In June 2015, Border Patrol agents, including BORTAC members, responded to assist the New York State Police in the manhunt for convicted murders Richard Matt and David Sweat, who had escaped from Dannemora Prison. On June 26, 2015, BORTAC member Chris Voss located and confronted an armed Richard Matt, resolving the situation by killing the escaped prisoner. David Sweat was captured by the New York State Police two days later.

On April 25, 2017, Carla Provost became the first female chief of the United States Border Patrol.

2020s

On February 4, 2020, President Donald Trump recognized the U.S. Border Patrol during the State of the Union Address.

In May–June 2020, Border Patrol agents responded to violent protests in Washington, DC, protecting federal buildings, including the White House.

In June 2020, Border Patrol agents deployed to Portland, Oregon, to provide riot control and protect federal buildings under attack by violent protesters.

On May 24, 2022, Border Patrol agents responded to the mass shooting at Robb Elementary School in Uvalde, Texas. Agents helped rescue/evacuate children, and BORTAC breached the classroom and terminated the shooter.

I think you can see from this storied history that the U.S. Border Patrol was, is, and continues to be the "Swiss Army knife" that is frequently called upon domestically and internationally to ensure the security and prosperity of the American people, our allies, and our friends. That is why serving as a Border Patrol agent was one of the most profoundly fulfilling things I have ever done in my life.

14

PATHS TO CITIZENSHIP

What motivated me to write this chapter was hearing the stories of people who have paid their life savings to coyotes to get them across the border. These stories tore at my heart because, in so many cases, if these people had been aware of the *legal* paths to U.S. citizenship, many would not have needed to risk their lives and their fortunes to try to cross into the United States illegally. What follows is a brief guide to the legal ways to enter, and in many cases become a citizen of, the United States.

Citizenship is the common thread that connects all Americans. It is a unique bond that unites people around civic ideals and a belief in the rights and freedoms guaranteed by the U.S. Constitution. We are a nation bound not by race or religion but by the shared values of freedom, liberty, and equality. Throughout our history, the United States has welcomed newcomers from all over the world. Immigrants have helped shape and define the country we know today. Their contributions help preserve our legacy as a land of freedom and opportunity. More than two hundred years after our founding, naturalized citizens have enriched our democracy.

Despite what is typically reported in the media, the United States is one of the most immigrant-friendly and welcoming nations on earth. This applies not only to the volume and diversity of immigrants absorbed by the U.S. every year but also to the multiple avenues an immigrant can take to obtain U.S. citizenship.

Although the U.S. immigration process may be complicated and feel counterintuitive for some, this can be said of any large bureaucratic process, and does not negate its validity or necessity. Anything of value worth obtaining is typically difficult to acquire, and in many cases part of the calculation of risk and reward is value through exclusion. Although this may appear to be a simplistic generalization, it is nevertheless true. For anyone reading this who thinks that the United States has lost its place in the world as the beacon of freedom and is no longer the shining city on the hill, I would suggest the following consideration as an antidote to any such notion.

When hundreds of thousands of people risk their lives to enter this country through the canyons, deserts, and rivers along our southern border, and thousands more spend their savings to travel across the world to become students, professionals, and skilled laborers in the United States, they are not encountering anyone going the other way.

It is also critical to establish certain factors to understand not only the process of obtaining U.S. citizenship but also certain terminology to reduce, if not eliminate, confusion. As discussed earlier, the U.S. immigration system is composed of numerous agencies operating under various legal doctrines and providing specific, but varied, services to the public. For the purposes of this explanation, the simplest approach is to divide them into enforcement agencies and administrative agencies.

The enforcement agencies are the law enforcement and immigration agencies operating in the United States to ensure that legal immigration and trade are facilitated, illegal immigration is prevented and mitigated at the border, and immigration enforcement takes place inside the United States. These agencies include Customs and Border Protection (Border Patrol, Air and Marine, Office of Field Operations) and Immigration and Customs Enforcement (ICE). Think of these agencies as the security personnel outside a concert arena or any other large venue. They are responsible for checking tickets, preventing weapons and other prohibited items from being smuggled in, generally ensuring that everyone behaves, and, in some cases, removing people who either circumvented the entry points and snuck in or who have violated some rule after being admitted. The enforcement agencies of our immigration system function in a similar fashion. They are responsible for protecting the physical borders of the United States and ensuring that anyone entering this country is properly identified and screened. Subsequently, they are also responsible for removing any individual who entered the country illegally or fraudulently.

The administrative agencies, on the other hand, are those that deal with establishing policies in accordance with immigration law and maintain a fair and equitable system for awarding, issuing, and processing visa requests. They are also responsible for processing other immigrant benefit claims, such as adjustments of status and naturalization petitions. These agencies would be the equivalent of the venue itself as well as the ticket-issuing company. The most crucial factor to remember is that the act of bestowing citizenship is a legal one, affirmed by a federal court, and is therefore predicated on the most important immigration principle of all: legal immigration.

Before discussing and defining immigration, it is important to understand the concept of citizenship. In the United States, there are two basic paths by which a person can obtain citizenship: *birth* or *naturalization*.

First, you can be born inside the United States or any of its legal territories and automatically become a citizen. Citizenship by birth also includes derived citizenship or transferred citizenship from parents. A child born to two U.S. citizens on vacation in France would still derive U.S. citizenship. Although there are some additional rules and restrictions involved in determining derived citizenship in cases where a child is born abroad to one or two U.S. citizen parents, the intent of this narrative is to provide a basic understanding of the immigration and naturalization process, not to dive into all the details.

The second path to citizenship is naturalization, a course of action that allows people to immigrate to the United States and become citizens. It also allows for anyone in the United States with a legal immigration status to petition for relatives living abroad to immigrate as well. This has been referred to as "chain migration," and it is the most common way for those not lucky enough to have won the geographic birth lottery to become U.S. residents and citizens. This principle of sponsorship applies in the same way that a current member of a private club could sponsor a nonmember for status and membership.

Now that we have defined the concepts guiding the acquisition of citizenship, it is important to discuss and clarify the most confused and misused element in the entire debate around immigration—the term itself.

Simply put, immigration is the transition of people from one country to another. This transition can either be temporary or permanent, and it can occur either legally or illegally. Legal immigration takes place through a formal request by a non-U.S. resident or citizen asking permission to enter the United States while living in another country. This process is done through U.S. embassies and consulates abroad and allows the U.S. government to properly vet and clear anyone attempting to visit or live in the United States.

Illegal immigration is the intentional circumvention of this legal immigration process where people either enter the United States between the official Ports of Entry without being inspected or entering in the United States legally but under false pretenses. The most common example of the first type of illegal immigration would be an individual crossing the Rio Grande along the southern border and being picked up and transported to the interior of the country. The most common example of the second type would be someone arriving on a tourist visa with the intention of living and working in the United States permanently. As I mentioned earlier, this is like being invited into one's home—

that invitation must be extended to the guest by the homeowner. Anyone arriving without an invitation and prior approval would be considered an intruder at worst and an inconvenience at best. Before inviting anyone into your home, you would also like to know how long they intend to stay. Obvious preparations and considerations must be made when considering if a guest will stay for several hours to enjoy dinner and drinks, sleep on your couch for a few nights while their home is being renovated, or intend to move into your basement and live with you and your family for the rest of their life.

The term *immigrant* applies to anyone who, in most cases, intends to abandon residency in their native country and permanently immigrate to the United States. Immigrant visas can be issued to anyone who is related to and is being sponsored by a U.S. citizen or permanent resident, someone who is married or engaged to be married to a U.S. citizen or resident, or someone who is seeking employment in the U.S.

There are also several other programs that allow for various religious workers as well as Iraqi and Afghan translators to apply for permanent residency and eventual citizenship. The final mechanism for immigrants is the Diversity Visa Program. Commonly referred to as a "visa lottery," the program is a way to allocate visas to countries around the world where a significant portion of the population is interested in immigrating to the United States. This program allows citizens of other countries to register their information for a visa. If selected under the diversity visa program, the individual and their family can apply and receive an immigrant visa to relocate to this country.

The term *nonimmigrant* applies to any individual who intends to enter the United States on a temporary basis. Although there are over two dozen categories of nonimmigrant visa, the most common are tourist visas, work visas, exchange program visas, NAFTA trade visas, and student visas. The holders of such visas are visitors who do not intend to live in the United States permanently, and are therefore not seeking citizenship.

Although the process of attaining citizenship may appear to be convoluted and less than streamlined, the actual steps in place are simple and straightforward. First, an individual must legally enter the United States as either an "intending immigrant" or, in some cases, a nonimmigrant who will later adjust their status. Second, they must become a permanent resident and live in the United States.

Residency requirements vary in certain cases, but as a rule one must live in the United States for five years. Finally, after meeting the above requirements, the immigrant can submit an application for naturalization. For anyone interested in a more in-depth explanation of the entire process, various free resources are available, including YouTube tutorials and resource pages from www.uscis.gov. When it comes to eligibility for U.S. citizenship, the most common paths are being related to a U.S. citizen, marrying a current U.S. citizen, serving in the U.S. military, or being a lawful permanent resident "green card" holder for a period of five years.

I am mindful that many people who want to immigrate to the United States speak Spanish; therefore, here is a translation into Spanish of this discussion of citizenship and immigration:

SPANISH TRANSLATION

Lo que me motivó a escribir este capítulo fue escuchar las historias de personas que les pagaron los ahorros de su vida a los coyotes para cruzar la frontera. Estas historias me desgarraron el corazón porque, en tantas situaciónes, si estas personas hubieran estado al tanto de los caminos *legales* hacia la ciudadanía estadounidense, muchos de ellos no habrían tenido que arriesgar sus vidas y sus fortunas para tratar de cruzar ilegalmente a los Estados Unidos. Lo que sigue es una breve guía sobre las formas legales de ingresar a este país y, en muchos casos, convertirse en ciudadano estadounidense.

La ciudadanía es el hilo común que conecta a todos los estadounidenses. Es un vínculo único que une a las personas en torno a los ideales cívicos y la creencia en los derechos y libertades garantizados por la Constitución de los Estados Unidos. Somos una nación unida no por la raza ni por la religión, sino por los valores compartidos de libertad e igualdad. A lo largo de nuestra historia, los Estados Unidos han recibido a recién llegados de todo el mundo. Los inmigrantes han ayudado a dar forma y definir el país que conocemos hoy. Sus contribuciones ayudan a preservar nuestro legado como una tierra de libertad y oportunidades. Más de doscientos años después de nuestra fundación, los ciudadanos naturalizados han enriquecido nuestra democracia.

A pesar de lo que típicamente se reporta en los medios de comunicación, los Estados Unidos es una de las naciones más amables y acogedoras del mundo hacia los inmigrantes. Esto no sólo se aplica al volumen y la diversidad de inmigrantes absorbidos por los EE. UU. cada año, sino también a las múltiples vías que un inmigrante pueda tomar para obtener la ciudadanía estadounidense.

Aunque el proceso de inmigración a los EE. UU. puede ser complicado y aparecer contradictorio para algunos, esto se puede decir de cualquier proceso burocrático grande, y no niega su validez ni su necesidad. Cualquier cosa de valor que valga la pena obtener suele ser difícil de adquirir y, en muchos casos, parte del cálculo de riesgo y recompensa es el valor por exclusión. Mientras parece ser una generalización simplista, no obstante, es cierto. Para cualquiera que lea esto y piense que los Estados Unidos han perdido su lugar en el mundo como el faro de la libertad y ya no es la ciudad brillante en la colina, sugeriría la siguiente consideración como antídoto a tal noción.

Cuando cientos de miles de personas arriesgan la vida para ingresar a este país a través de los cañones, desiertos, y ríos a lo largo de nuestra frontera sur, y miles más gastan sus ahorros para viajar por el mundo para convertirse en estudiantes, profesionales, y trabajadores calificados en los Estados Unidos, no se encuentran con nadie que vaya en sentido contrario.

Es fundamental establecer ciertos factores no sólo para comprender el proceso de adquirir la ciudadanía estadounidense, sino también para comprender cierta terminología para reducir, si no eliminar, la confusión. Como se discutió anteriormente, el sistema de inmigración de los EE. UU. está compuesto por numerosas agencias que operan bajo diversas doctrinas legales y brindan servicios específicos, pero variados, al público. Para el propósito de esta explicación, el método más sencillo es dividirlas en agencias de ejecución y agencias administrativas.

Las agencias de ejecución que operan en los Estados Unidos son las de aplicación de la ley y de inmigración para garantizar 1) que se facilite la inmigración legal y el comercio, 2) que se prevenga y mitigue la inmigración ilegal en la frontera, y 3) que la imposición de leyes migraorias se lleve a cabo dentro del país. Estas agencias incluyen Aduanas y Protección Fronteriza (Patrulla Fronteriza, Aire y Marina, Oficina de Operaciones de Campo) e Inmigración y Control de Aduanas (ICE). Piense en estas agencias como el personal de seguridad fuera de una arena de conciertos o cualquier otro sitio grande. Son los encargados de 1) controlar las entradas, 2) evitar el contrabando de armas y otros artículos prohibidos, 3) velar generalmente por el buen comportamiento de todos, y 4) en algunos casos, sacar a las personas que so colaron mediante sortear los puntos de entrada o que infringieron alguna regla después de ser admitidos. Las agencias de ejecución de nuestro sistema de inmigración funcionan de manera similar. Son responsables de proteger las fronteras físicas de los Estados Unidos y garantizar que cualquier persona que ingrese a este país esté debidamente identificada y filtrada. Posteriormente, también son responsables de expulsar a cualquier persona que haya ingresado al país ilegalmente o de modo fradulento.

Por otro lado, las agencias administrativas se encargan de establecer las políticas según la ley migratoria y de mantener un sistema justo y equitativo para otorgar, distribuir, y procesar las peticiones de las visas. También se encargan de controlar otras prestaciones migratorias, como las peticiones para la naturalización o para ajustar el estatus. Estas agencias serían equivalentes a la dirección del sitio mismo o al servicio de venta de boletos. El elemento más crítico para tener en cuenta es que el otorgar la ciudadanía es un acto legal, afirmado por el tribunal federal, y por lo tanto establecido en el principio migratorio más importante: la inmigración legal.

Antes de discutir y definir la inmigración, es importante entender el concepto de ciudadanía. En los Estados Unidos existen dos caminos básicos por los cuales una persona puede obtener la ciudadanía: mediante el nacimiento o mediante la naturalización.

Si uno nació en los Estados Unidos o unos de sus territorios legales, automáticamente es ciudadano. Este tipo de ciudadanía también incluye ciudadanía derivada o ciudadanía transferida de los padres. Un niño nacido de dos padres ciudadanos estadounidenses que están en Francia de vacaciones, aún obtendría la ciudadanía estadounidense. Aunque existen algunas reglas y restricciones para determinar la ciudadanía derivada en los casos en que un niño nace en el extranjero de uno o dos padres ciudadanos estadounidenses, la intención de este discurso es proveer una comprensión básica del proceso de inmigración y naturalización, no es elaborar todos los detalles.

El segundo camino a la ciudadanía es la naturalización, un acto que permite que las personas inmigren a los Estados Unidos y se conviertan en ciudadanos. De igual forma, permite que cualquier persona en los Estados Unidos con un estatus migratorio legal haga una petición para que sus familiares, que viven en el extranjero, puedan inmigrar a los Estados Unidos. Esto se ha denominado "migración en cadena" y es la forma más común de convertirse en residentes y ciudadanos de los EE. UU.

para las personas que no tuvieron la suerte de haber ganado la lotería geográfica del nacimiento. Este principio de patrocinio es parecido a un club privado que permite que un miembro actual patrocine a un no miembro para obtener estatus y membresía.

Ahora que hemos definido los conceptos que guían la adquisición de la ciudadanía, es importante hablar sobre y aclarar la terminología más confusa y mal utilizada en todo el debate sobre la inmigración—el término en sí.

En pocas palabras, la inmigración es la transición de personas de un país a otro. Esta transición puede ser temporal o permanente, y puede ocurrir de manera legal o ilegal. La inmigración legal se lleva a cabo a través de una solicitud formal de un ciudadano o residente no estadounidense que solicita permiso para ingresar a los Estados Unidos mientras vive en otro país. Este proceso se realiza por medio de las embajadas y los consulados estadounidenses en el extranjero y permite que el gobierno de los EE. UU. investigue y autorice adecuadamente a cualquier persona que intente visitar o vivir en los Estados Unidos.

La inmigración ilegal es la elusión intencional de este proceso de inmigración legal donde las personas ingresan a los Estados Unidos mediante los puertos de entrada oficiales sin ser inspeccionadas, o ingresan a los Estados Unidos legalmente pero bajo falsos pretextos. El ejemplo más común del primer tipo de inmigración ilegal sería una persona que es recogida y transportada al interior del país después de cruzar el Río Grande a lo largo de la frontera sur. El ejemplo más común del segundo tipo sería una persona que llega con una visa de turista con la intención de vivir y trabajar en el los Estados Unidos. Como se mencionó anteriormente, esto es como una invitación a la casa de alguien. Para ser recibido, el propietario debe extender una invitación al huésped. Si alguien llega sin una invitación y aprobación previa, sería considerado un intruso en el peor de los casos y un inconveniente en el mejor de los casos. Antes de invitar a alguien a su casa, también se debe saber por cuánto tiempo piensa quedarse. Se deben hacer preparativos y consideraciones obvias al considerar si un huésped se quedará durante varias horas para disfrutar de una cena y bebidas, si dormirá en su sofá por algunas noches mientras se renueva su casa, o si intentará mudarse a su sótano y vivir con usted y su familia por el resto de su vida.

Así como existe la inmigración legal e ilegal, también existe la inmigración permanente y temporal. Esto es a menudo donde se produce la confusión y la apropiación indebida de los términos. Los Estados Unidos generalmente clasifican a cualquier persona que llega al país como inmigrante o no inmigrante. Obviamente, esto excluye alguien que sea residente permanente o ciudadano de los Estados Unidos y simplemente regrese de un viaje corto al extranjero.

El término *inmigrante* se aplica a cualquier persona que, en la mayoría de los casos, tiene la intención de abandonar su residencia en su país de origen y inmigrar permanentemente a los Estados Unidos. Las visas de inmigrante se pueden emitir a cualquier persona que esté relacionada con un ciudadano o residente permanente de los EE. UU. y esté patrocinada por él, alguien que esté casado o comprometido para casarse con un ciudadano o residente de los EE. UU., o alguien que esté buscando empleo en los Estados Unidos.

También hay otros programas que permiten que varios trabajadores religiosos y traductores iraquíes y afganos soliciten la residencia permanente y la ciudadanía en los Estados Unidos. El último mecanismo para inmigrantes es el Programa de Visas de Diversidad. Comúnmente conocida como "lotería de visas," es una forma en que los Estados Unidos asigna visas a países de todo el mundo donde una parte significativa de la población está interesada en inmigrar a los Estados Unidos. Este programa permite que los ciudadanos de otros países registren su información para una visa a los Estados Unidos. Si es seleccionado bajo el programa, la persona y su familia pueden solicitar y recibir una visa de inmigrante para mudarse a este país.

El término *no inmigrante* se aplica a cualquier persona que tenga la intención de ingresar a los Estados Unidos de forma temporal. Aunque hay más de dos docenas de categorías de visas de no inmigrante, las más comunes son: visas de turista, visas de trabajo, visas de programas de intercambio, visas comerciales NAFTA, y visas de estudiante. Estos son esencialmente visitantes y no tienen la intención de vivir en los Estados Unidos de forma permanente y, por lo tanto, no buscan la ciudadanía.

Aunque el proceso de obtener la ciudadanía parece complicado y no simplificado, los pasos reales son sencillos y directos. Primero, una persona debe ingresar legalmente a los Estados Unidos como "inmigrante potencial" o, en algunos casos, como no inmigrante para luego ajustar su estatus. Segundo, debe convertirse en residente permanente y vivir en los Estados Unidos.

Los requisitos de residencia varían en ciertos casos, pero por regla general, una persona debe vivir en los Estados Unidos por cinco años. Finalmente, luego de cumplir con los requisitos anteriores, la persona puede presentar una solicitud de naturalización. Si alguien está interesado en una explicación más detallada de todo el proceso, hay varios recursos gratuitos disponibles, incluidos tutoriales de YouTube y páginas de recursos de www.uscis.gov. Cuando se trata de la elegibilidad para la ciudadanía estadounidense, los caminos más comunes incluyen el ser relacionado con un ciudadano estadounidense, casarse con un ciudadano estadounidense actual, servir en el ejército de los EE. UU., o ser titular de una "tarjeta verde" de residente permanente legal por un período de cinco años.

15

A CAREER WITH BREATHTAKING POSSIBILITIES

Throughout this book you have not only read stories about my time as a Border Patrol agent but also gained more general information about the roles and responsibilities of agents as they work to defend our nation. You may also have been inspired to consider joining the agency yourself.

I don't want to oversell becoming a Border Patrol agent. It is not a professional vocation that is right for everyone. This chapter is designed to tell you what wearing the uniform means and what you can expect from your fellow agents.

The best way to highlight the agency's inherent sense of adventure comes directly from our organization. Here is how the Border Patrol website puts it:

ADRENALINE RUSHES COME STANDARD

Border Patrol Agents: The primary mission of the Border Patrol is to protect our Nation by reducing the likelihood that dangerous people and capabilities enter the

United States between the Ports of Entry. Border Patrol Agents sit squarely on the front lines, guarding our country from illegal activity while providing aid to those in need. It's mentally and physically challenging and requires both courage and compassion. If you are looking for a rewarding job that also provides great pay, benefits and job stability, join our team.

The people I served with during my days as a Border Patrol agent had this as their organizing impulse, and these are the kind of people who are protecting your borders at this very moment. I'd like to tell you a bit more about them as they work to fulfill the Border Patrol's priority mission of preventing terrorists and terrorist weapons, including weapons of mass destruction, from entering the United States and detecting and preventing the illegal entry of individuals into the United States.

I don't know why I remember this, but I recall that Benjamin Disraeli once said: "There are three kinds of lies: lies, damned lies, and statistics." I am not a big fan of statistics, and I am guessing that most of you reading this book didn't pick it up to be bludgeoned by pages of mind-numbing numbers, graphs, or pie charts.

That said, as I developed my narrative for this book, I realized that it would be helpful to use some really basic numbers to help explain who the people are who guard your borders today. So here are the numbers that I think best tell that story. Don't worry; there aren't any equations that you have to solve.

First, by way of introduction and perhaps leveling the playing field, most people agree that the majority of organizations or professions benefit from diversity. The U.S. military has a long history of fostering diversity in its ranks as it draws from a large talent pool of candidates to become potential soldiers, sailors, airmen, and Marines.

Most organizations—especially government entities—say, and I think truthfully, that they want their outfit to "look like America." In other words, they want their demographics—gender, race, age, lifestyle, etc.—to mirror those of America's population. Depending on the organization or profession, this is often easier said than done. The Border Patrol has worked hard to "look like America" and has largely succeeded.

There are approximately twenty thousand Border Patrol agents serving today. Men make up 86 percent of the total, while women make up 14 percent. By way of reference, this is roughly the same percentage as the U.S. military. The most common ethnicity of Border Patrol agents is white (65 percent), followed by Hispanic or Latino (20 percent) and Black or African American (8 percent). Of the total, 6 percent of agents self-identify as LGBT. You may find it surprising—given the arduous nature of patrolling the hot and barren southern border—that the average age of the Border Patrol is just north of forty. All of these numbers have remained remarkably steady over the past decade.

In previous chapters I told you about the challenging academic aspects of the Border Patrol Academy. That is why highly educated people make up a substantial portion of Border Patrol agents: 5 percent have a master's degree, over 60 percent have a bachelor's degree, and 20 percent have an associate's degree.

I believe the pay and benefits of working for the federal government are what attracts many—and I am one of them—to serve as a Border Patrol agent. You won't get rich as an agent, but you can carve out a comfortable life for your family.

Depending on your education and experience, you have two primary paths to choose from to serve as a Border Patrol agent. You enter as a GS-5, GS-7, or GS-9. (GS refers to "Government Service" and pay grades represent different levels of compensation. A rough analogy would be military pay grades where a sergeant makes more money than a corporal, who makes more than a private.) As a GS-7 moves up in time in service, he or she has a base salary of $43,000. Add overtime and premium pay and that rises to $70,000. For a GS-9, the numbers are higher, a base salary of $48,000, and overtime and premium pay that increases the total to $80,000. That's not a bad living.

Those with aspirations to take on leadership, management, or supervisory roles can strive to enter higher pay scales as a GS-13, 14, or 15, and some of those men and women can ultimately be part of the Senior Executive Service with salaries pushing close to $200,000. Added to all this is a generous benefits package of health insurance, life insurance, tuition assistance, paid leave, and retirement credits.

For those of you currently in the military who are looking for a potential career outside of active duty that aligns similarly, the Border Patrol has a long list of different career fields you can venture into once you have completed your entry-level time.

The scope of career paths is, in a word, *breathtaking*. Here is just a short summary:

HORSE PATROL: The Horse Patrol program is composed of skilled horse riders, trainers, and instructors. Horse Patrol agents ride in challenging, environmentally protected, and privately owned sensitive geographic locations and terrain. The Horse Patrol are the most viable, and, in some cases, the only option for the U.S. Border Patrol to use when entering regions inaccessible by any other means, such as 4 × 4 or all-terrain vehicles (ATVs). Without the Horse Patrol, these areas would remain unpatrolled and susceptible to transnational criminal activity.

BIKE PATROL: The Bike Patrol operations facilitate the apprehension of all cross-border threats by utilizing the unique tactical law enforcement advantages of stealth, mobility, agility, and accessibility.

K-9 UNIT: The K-9 Unit uses canines to detect concealed humans and odors of narcotics. The unit also performs search and rescue, special response patrol, human remains detection, and tracking/trailing.

BOAT PATROL: Patrol boats are used to access the water boundaries of the United States. Specially trained agents use airboats, shallow-draft vessels, and V-hull platforms to patrol remote waterways and otherwise inaccessible landings that could be exploited by criminal smuggling elements without a law enforcement presence.

OFF-ROAD VEHICLE UNIT: The Off-Road Vehicle Unit is composed of specially trained agents that use different off-road packaged vehicles, such as ATVs, dirt bikes, and other vehicles, specifically designed to secure inaccessible areas of the border and intercept drug runners and undocumented noncitizens.

BORDER PATROL SEARCH, TRAUMA, AND RESCUE (BORSTAR): The BORSTAR Unit provides law enforcement, search and rescue, and medical response capabilities for the U.S. Border Patrol. Additionally, BORSTAR provides mutual assistance to local, county, state, tribal, and federal entities by responding to enforcement and search-and-rescue requirements, acts of terrorism, potential terrorism, and natural disasters throughout the United States.

BORDER PATROL TACTICAL UNIT (BORTAC): BORTAC provides the Department of Homeland Security with a highly trained and specially equipped tactical unit for specialized rapid response or deliberate deployments to law enforcement situations and intelligence-based threats requiring special tactics, techniques, and procedures in defense of our national security.

MOBILE RESPONSE TEAM (MRT): The Mobile Response Team provides a national group of organized, trained, and equipped Border Patrol agents capable of rapid movement to regional and national incidents in support of priority CBP operations. MRT provides a flexible and enhanced tiered-response capability to counter the emerging, changing, and evolving threats in our most challenging operational areas along our nation's borders.

HONOR GUARD: The USBP Honor Guard is a unit of volunteer agents whose primary duty is to render final honors and conduct memorial services for law enforcement personnel who die in the line of duty. The Honor Guard is composed of a cross section of members, some of whom are Pipes and Drum members, which are Great Highland bagpipers or Scottish-style drummers. The USBP Honor Guard and Pipes and Drums have placed well in and won numerous competitions.

PEER SUPPORT PROGRAM (PSP): The PSP offers confidential assistance and support to all U.S. Border Patrol employees and their family members in times of personal need or due to traumatic incidents. The PSP works in conjunction with the Employee Assistance Program (EAP) and does not replace psychological treatment. The objective of the PSP is to minimize psychological trauma that Border Patrol employees and their families may experience throughout their careers and render assistance in an attempt to accelerate normal recovery to abnormal events, some of which are unique to the Border Patrol environment.

NATIONAL PISTOL TEAM: The National Pistol Team continues to strive for excellence and to exemplify what well-trained Border Patrol agents can accomplish with a firearm. The legacy of Border Patrol shooters consists of some of the most famous law enforcement officers of the early twentieth century and the most decorated competitors of three different shooting sports. All of this has been accomplished almost entirely by field agents assigned to non-firearms-related Border Patrol duties. The USBP National Pistol Team has dominated National Police Shooting Championship contests. Since 1966, ten Border Patrol agents have won a national championship.

FIREARMS INSTRUCTOR TRAINING PROGRAM: This program is dedicated to delivering the highest-caliber firearms training and education and continually seeks the most effective and innovative training methods. Firearms instructors train and certify agents, arming them with the fundamental knowledge and skills required to conduct CBP operations located throughout the world.

LESS-LETHAL INSTRUCTOR TRAINING PROGRAM: This program educates, trains, and certifies tactical instructors who deliver mission-specific training to CBP personnel, as well as to national and international partners. The training programs continually evolve and advance to encompass the tools, tactics, mindset, and methodologies needed to engage the ever-changing threats to our nation.

EMERGENCY MEDICAL PROGRAM (EMP): The U.S. Border Patrol EMP is composed of certified emergency medical technicians (EMTs) and paramedics who provide emergency medical response and training to the U.S. Border Patrol. The EMP responds to a vast array of emergencies that range from medical illnesses to traumatic injuries. EMP personnel are highly trained in emergency medicine and use their skills to save lives and treat the injuries of fellow agents, illegal aliens, and people from the communities in which they serve.

CHAPLAINCY: The primary purpose of the Chaplaincy Program is promoting the well-being of the U.S. Border Patrol workforce. Chaplains provide guidance for both physical and mental health, including stress management. The Chaplaincy Program provides educational resources and training on difficult topics, including suicide prevention and awareness and law enforcement–related stress. The Chaplaincy Program also provides connections to local community resources.

You can easily see from the list above why the Border Patrol attracts so many candidates. Border Patrol agents have a vast array of options to choose from to find a role that suits their talents and aspirations, all while allowing them to perform a mission of vital national importance. But beyond each Border Patrol agent's unique role, there is an overarching culture that comprises *who we are*.

16

DEL RIO SPECIAL OPERATIONS INVOLVEMENT AT ROBB ELEMENTARY IN UVALDE, TEXAS

In this chapter, I have collected accounts and constructed a time-line that represents what happened on May 24, 2022, when an active shooter infiltrated Robb Elementary School in Uvalde, Texas. I have retrieved information from open sources as well as from local journalists who wish to remain anonymous. On that day, the Del Rio BORSTAR and BORTAC teams woke up and reported to their work areas as they normally did. They didn't imagine they would become heroes who would save lives that day.

The Eagle Pass North area of operations is currently the most trafficked area in the nation. Agents who work the day shift (early morning shift before the sun comes up) have the advantage of beating the heat and stopping as much traffic as possible before the illegal border crossers load up their contra-band. BORSTAR agents were working the groups in the same fashion I did when I was there. Tracking K-9's are affected by the heat. Their nose effectiveness and their drive drop dramatically. BORSTAR had been actively using Black Hawk air assets to help with apprehensions. Unfortunately, the Black Hawk assigned for that week was canceled due to a mechanical issue. This was especially unfortunate as the Black Hawk might have helped transport the agents to Uvalde.

Sven Crocker's brush crew was working a camera activation on the Roswell ranch near FM481, Eagle Pass. They had been working the group and were nearing their load-up spot when a BORSTAR team helped them round up the group. At approximately 1140, a call came over the radio net: "All available units head to Robb Elementary; there is an active shooter." The radio went quiet for a second before an agent came on and asked if they could repeat the traffic. Uvalde agents weren't familiar with the area schools, and one agent asked where Robb Elementary was located. A seasoned agent stated over the radio that it was the school closest to the "Old Dickies Plant on Highway 83." That was a known landmark that the agents could use to navigate. Once the Special Operations units were notified, they made their way to Uvalde to try and help with the active shooter situation. Several BORSTAR operators knew Uvalde and attended Robb Elementary when they were young.

It took the BORSTAR agents forty-five minutes to arrive on scene. The area was extremely congested, not only from law enforcement responding to the call but also from parents fighting to get to their kids.

A call on the radio stated that the suspect had gone into the building and had barricaded himself in. The teams prepped their gear, suited up their armor, rifles, and medical gear, and grabbed handfuls of tourniquets. They ran toward the school, guided by law enforcement officers, including DPS, game wardens, and local police. They were shown the door where the shooter had made entry into the school.

Once arriving in the building, the acting BORTAC commander linked up with the BORSTAR team to assess the situation. Surrounding law enforcement officers were told that the doors to the classroom behind which the gunman had barricaded himself were locked and that the doors opened outward. To top it off, they were metal doors. A rumor circulated that someone was trying to negotiate with the shooter.

By this time, the shooter had already fired over one hundred rounds inside the classroom. This was information the BORTAC and BORSTAR team wasn't privy to. After a review of cameras and timelines, it was later found that the chief was at the opposite end of the hallway and never talked to the shooter. The BORTAC commander was told that if officers approached the door, the shooter would begin firing.

BORSTAR paramedics were working with Uvalde Border Patrol EMTs by setting up a triage area with all available medical equipment. BORTAC snipers attempted to get into a location of advantage, but the windows they were hoping to have a line of sight to were covered.

By this time BORTAC members decided to make entry into the classroom, where they were met with accurate engagement by the shooter. BORTAC agents were successful in their efforts to neutralize the shooter, and received only minor injuries.

Therefore, the next task was to provide medical intervention for as many teachers and children as possible.

The reports about the casualties were accurate and hard to comprehend. I will not describe in graphic detail the situation the BORSTAR agents confronted because it is too horrific. It is indescribable and unfathomable that another human being was capable of such cruelty. The BORSTAR team and the Uvalde Border Patrol EMTs and the EMTs who transported the children that day will forever have those images burned into their memories.

I know this because I live with a similar memory from Afghanistan. I feel for those who have been affected by this terrible event in any way, shape, or form. I am also honored to have worked side by side with the BORSTAR agents, many of whom I have mentioned in previous chapters, who were on the ground that day trying to save every life they could. They live by a motto to serve the people of the United States of America.

ERIGERE RAPIDUS
SO OTHERS MAY LIVE

AFTERWORD

In most books of this type, the afterword is brief, and this one will be as well. And while this is something you all will read, it is meant primarily as a shout-out to my fellow Border Patrol agents, past, present, and future.

I wanted to write this message to let you know that there are many millions of Americans that support your efforts. We understand the hardships you face and the lack of appreciation.

A Journeyman once told me that the career of a Border Patrol agent comes in waves. Sometimes things are bad, but eventually they get better. Since I was in, I've seen that multiple times.

And I've found this to be true. Yes, right now, in your profession, you might feel down, even way down. Please don't forget that what you do matters. It may seem like it's pointless at times and daunting given the lack of support and often negative media, but it matters.

You have to keep the positives in perspective. Do you catch everything coming across the border? No. But with the narcotics you *do* stop at the border, how many overdose deaths do you think you've prevented? The number could only be one, but that's enough for me. Knowing that a family doesn't have to go through the heartbreak of losing a loved one (most often a young loved one) all because an agent was doing his job should be enough of a reward for all of us.

We see it all too often when Border Patrol apprehends a sex offender, a wanted criminal, and others who are a blight on society. Knowing that these individuals are stopped before they can cause havoc in our communities is a win for us any day.

The hard truth is that every agent knows the border is not completely secure and never truly will be. We can't stop illegal immigration or the flow of narcotics completely. But we hold the line against the tide regardless.

This is what you do, and it is who you are. Regardless of who sits in the White House or who the Border Patrol chief is, you are on watch every day around the clock. You do the job to protect our country, our communities, and our brothers/sisters who hold that line.

I know all too well that being a Border Patrol agent is often a dangerous and thankless job. It has always been that way. But consider the countless people you save, as well as the lives you impact in so many positive ways—that is enough to reinforce the fact that you are in a righteous profession. It will always be enough.

When you seize fentanyl, meth, or other illicit drugs, I know that doesn't stop people from buying it. But if you stopped even one overdose, that is more than enough for me. I know in my former sector they have caught plenty of criminals, especially sex offenders. Knowing that you have stopped those monsters and saved small children from that hell is a priceless feeling. You have to take the victories as they come.

I have watched Del Rio Sector get bashed and ridiculed, and I have been trying to find some words of encouragement that would be impactful, but I can only compare what you are going through with questions veterans often receive: "Why did you do it? Why are we even over there?"

Most people will never understand why we served; everyone served in the military for their own reasons. Some did it for patriotism, others did it for college benefits, and some even did it for the dental plan. Either way, in combat no one is thinking of those initial reasons. We are all thinking only about the person to the left and the right of us, we don't think about politics or whether or not we are there for the right reasons. In those moments we are fighting just for our brothers and sisters in uniform.

This quote from the movie *Black Hawk Down* is probably the most honest dialogue I have heard in a military film.

Hoot: "When I go home brothers ask me, 'Hey Hoot, why do you do it man? What, you some kinda war junkie?' You know what I'll say? I won't say a goddamn word. Why? They won't understand. They won't understand why we do it. They won't understand that it's about the men next to you, and that's it. That's all it is."

I would tell you it is no different in the Patrol. We cannot control the political climate; we cannot be discouraged by the misinformation that is spread in the media and their efforts to use the Border Patrol as the scapegoat.

I know that my fellow countrymen—those who are informed—have a deep sense of appreciation for what the Border Patrol does. I have an enormous sense of pride for each and every one of my brothers and sisters who wears the badge. I am proud of what we do because I truly know what it is we do, even if pundits and the media do not. I think back to the good I have done and the good we continue to do.

Can it be difficult? Clearly. But I am proud of what we do. I know that many individuals I have encountered have been treated with courtesy and respect. I can focus on only the positive; that is what we must do. Outside actors will never understand what we truly do. Knowing the good we have done—and will continue to do—is enough. The rest is just noise.

ACKNOWLEDGMENTS

As America's thirty-fifth president, John Fitzgerald Kennedy, famously said: "Victory has a thousand fathers, but defeat is an orphan." The fact that you are reading this book about the Border Patrol is a testimony to the fact that in my journey to be the best person, son, father, and Border Patrol agent, there were many, many fathers and mothers who helped me along this path.

First, my family. I am mindful that I recognized my immediate family in this book's dedication, but that surfs the wave tops. There are other family members I must mention.

To my family in El Paso, I love you. I am always hoping I am making you all proud. To my family in Los Angeles and a few that moved across several states, I love you. I hope I make the Vargas name proud. I know we aren't as close as we were when we were young, but I will always be here for you.

To my in-laws: When Christie and I got married, I was blessed to have been gifted with you in my life. I want to express my gratitude for your unwavering support. It means more to me than you will ever understand.

To María Isabel Medina Amador, thank you for your professionalism and the translation in chapter 14.

The U.S. military services are well-known for many things, but near the top of that list is mentoring, with seniors teaching juniors not only how to march and shoot straight but also a host of life skills. I must thank the 75th Ranger Regiment for the foundation they laid when sculpting my mind, body, and spirit. The Ranger Creed will forever be woven into the fabric of my character.

As it is in the U.S. military, mentoring is an important aspect of the Border Patrol, and it is a crucial component of making it what it has become today. Past and present Border Patrol professionals who have helped me become an agent include: 880 from Del Rio! My brothers and sisters. Every letter spilled onto this page was an effort to protect you and your families. To be the voice for so many that don't have the same privileges I do. We shared laughs and tears. I will never forget my time with you.

To Eagle Pass North Station and Del Rio Sector, I am proud to have been a part of your history. I hope I continue to make you proud. I know the boxing and softball teams will never be the same without me. LOL, Echo THREEEEEEE SEVEEEEEEN FIIIIIVE OUT!

To Joe Banco, author of *Honor First: The Story of the United*

States Border Patrol, thank you for contributing to this book. Keep telling the world about our history.

To El Centro Sector Strategic Communications Branch, thank you for being an influential force that will help our communities for many years. Your talents far surpass anything I could ever imagine. I appreciate your efforts.

To Leon Landa, the brain I needed when crafting a message. I appreciate your contribution to reading my thoughts and cleaning up the rough edges of my Border Patrol knowledge. This book wouldn't be what it is without your help.

To my Special Operations family: BORTAC and especially BORSTAR. It was an honor to serve with you. Every day I regret leaving. I miss you. I would still die for any one of you. Keep up the fight, I am incredibly proud of all of you.

HONOR FIRST / SO OTHERS MAY LIVE

To Jocko Willink, this all started with you. I am always in awe of your humility and willingness to support my efforts. I won't let you down.

To my agent, Jennifer Joel, thank you for believing in this project and being a partner in this venture. Without your support, this wouldn't have been a thing. I promise there is more in this head I need to get out. Stand by.

To Marc Resnick, thank you for the motivation and support. It's an honor to work with someone of your stature. I hope to make you proud, and that we can build on this project.

Tom MacDonald: For supplying the music, I kept it on repeat while writing this.

Devin: December 16, 2005—you earned your tab the day I did. You were my motivation. I miss your smile and hilarious stories.

SSG Ricardo Barraza: Your influence pours through me for others to follow. This is because of your dedication to the mission and the country. I only hope I have made you proud. I get embarrassed by how often I think of and mention you. I feel silly about how much time has passed and how much I am still emotionally affected by hearing your name. I now think about how proud I am to have known you. It's been the most impactful influence in my life.

INDEX